101 Questions and Answers on Vatican II

101 Questions and Answers on Vatican II

Maureen Sullivan, O.P.

PAULIST PRESS
New York/Mahwah, N.J.

All quotations from Vatican II's documents contained herein are from Walter Abbott, ed., *Documents of Vatican II,* copyright 1966 by America Press, and are reprinted with permission of America Press.

The Scripture quotations contained herein are from the New Revised Standard Version Bible, copyright 1989 by the Division of Christian Education of the National Council of the Churches of Christ in the U.S.A. and are used by permission. All rights reserved.

Book design by Theresa M. Sparacio

Cover design by Cynthia Dunne

Library of Congress Cataloging-in-Publication Data

Sullivan, Maureen, O.P.
101 questions and answers on Vatican II / Maureen Sullivan.
p. cm.
Includes bibliographical references.
ISBN 0-8091-4133-7
1. Vatican Council (2nd : 1962–1965). I. Title: One hundred and one. II. Title: One hundred one. III. Title
BX830 1962 .O88 2002
262′.52—dc21

2002012511

Published by Paulist Press
997 Macarthur Boulevard
Mahwah, New Jersey 07430

www.paulistpress.com

Printed and bound in the
United States of America

CONTENTS

Dedication

For my parents, Eileen and Lawrence,
from whom I learned the meaning of the line:
*You know very well that love is, above all,
the gift of oneself. (Jean Anouilh)*

Acknowledgments

Thanks to my sisters Patricia, Eileen, and Margaret and their families—the Carranos, the Petronios, the Poggis. From them I have learned to love more and laugh often.

Thanks to Gloria and Mary Lisa. From them I have learned that friends can provide what no one else can. They have blessed my life.

Thanks to my religious congregation, the Dominican Sisters of Hope. From them I received my appreciation for the Dominican charism of study and the opportunity to pursue it.

Thanks to my colleagues at St. Anselm College. From them I received encouragement and good example in my theological journey.

Thanks to my students at St. Anselm College. They have listened to my stories, laughed at my jokes, and given me their friendship. They have opened their minds and hearts to theology and have convinced me that the church of the twenty-first century will be safe in their hands.

Thanks to Linda Bradley and Denise LaRoche. From them I learned that secretaries are very special people.

Thanks to the William H. Sadlier Publishing Company. From them I have been given countless opportunities to speak to the people of God in presentations all over the United States.

Thanks to Gerald O'Collins, S.J. From him I received the inspiration to write this book.

Thanks to Robert Blair Kaiser. From him in particular I learned so much about Vatican II. He generously shared his knowledge, his enthusiasm, and his friendship. He made me believe I had a story to tell and convinced me that I had the ability to tell it.

Thanks to Christopher Bellitto, my editor and friend at Paulist Press. From him I received what every writer needs—encouragement, support, regular feedback, and incredibly clear recommendations!

And finally, a very special thanks to Blessed John XXIII for the gift that he *was* by his life and for the gift that he *gave* to the human family, the Second Vatican Council.

INTRODUCTION

I knew the church before Vatican II, as an elementary and high school student in New York City, and I have known the church as a member of the Dominican Sisters of Hope, which I entered in August of 1965, just as Vatican II was drawing to a close.

My early years provided me with what many would call the "catechism mentality." I had all the answers, often enough before I really understood the questions, but that early training served me well because it gave me a solid foundation in Catholic tradition. More importantly, I think, it provided me with a background for understanding the new charter for the church that was being developed by the Fathers of the Council.

I built on that background during my years as a religious. I was a Dominican, and so was St. Thomas Aquinas, a man who spent his whole life in a quest to understand his faith. And so it was in the Dominican intellectual tradition, then, that my mentors in the Order moved quite naturally to help me realize in the deepest ways what the church was up to during Vatican II when it tried to re-think and re-form some of its most ancient understandings in and for a world that had suddenly "come of age." In fact, some of the Council's leading theologians were Dominican. I am thinking of Father Yves Congar from France, an expert on the history of the church, Father M. D. Chenu, also from France, another church historian, and Father Edward Schillebeeckx from the Netherlands, an expert on the history of the sacraments, Dominicans all.

The Council was launched forty years ago. Some commentators have said it was the most significant event in the history of the church since Pentecost, when the Holy Spirit sent tongues of fire down upon the apostles, and prompted them to carry the good news to every land on earth. Others have said the Council attempted to reverse a thousand years of history, to reform and renew a Catholicism that had become almost as outmoded as the oxcart.

The sad fact is that few Catholics who are alive today really understand what the Council was all about. Back in the 1960s and 1970s some fine books were published on Vatican II, but they are now out of print. The conciliar documents themselves are still in print, but many have found them dense and difficult to read. A current history being produced by a team of scholars centered in Bologna seems aimed at scholars (and at a scholarly price as well). There have been a number of fine novels written about World War I and World War II. But no writer has produced a good novel about Vatican II.

At the very least, the world would hail a popular history of the Council that mines all the memoirs of all those who were there. In a sense, you had to be there to fully realize what was happening. Even for those who were there, understanding dawned slowly. Denis Hurley, the Archbishop of Durban, South Africa, said in an October 2000 interview that not even he saw the Council's significance in the beginning. He said that he had to learn, little by little, during the course of the Council's four years, though he was a member of the commission of bishops who helped prepare for the Council. For Hurley, the Council was "the biggest, most famous, historic adult education project ever held." That education came, he said, when the bishops at the Council sat at the feet of the church's scriptural scholars, theologians, and historians to learn how they could help restore "the simple and pure lines that the face of the Church of Jesus had at its birth." (The quote comes from a speech delivered before the Council by Blessed Pope John XXIII.)

When many of those bishops came home from the Council, they had a hard time explaining to their own priests (and their own people) that the Council had fashioned a new charter for the church. Preconciliar Catholics had been taught to look upon the church as a mighty answer machine. When some heard their bishops speak about the church as the pilgrim people of God, a people always in search of the fullness of truth, they felt confused and disillusioned. Some were bewildered. This was not the know-everything church they grew up with. They were puzzled by a church that said it was still searching for the truth. Many priests and nuns (and a good many laypeople) went into denial and reverted to the preconciliar model of a church that was sure of itself. Some demanded Mass in Latin. Some (even some cardinals in Rome) repudiated the Council.

The time is right for another book—a popular primer on Vatican II that will help bring everything into focus and show that the Council's charter is not a dead letter, but a piece of history that still lives and inspires the most serious Christians on the planet. The editors at Paulist Press might well have called this *Everything You Wanted to Know about the Council, but Were Afraid to Ask Because You Feared It Might Change Your Life.*

I am a professor at St. Anselm College in Manchester, New Hampshire, with a doctorate in theology from the Jesuits at Fordham University. So you will not be surprised to know that I take my religion seriously. Imagine my distress these days when I find students enrolling in my courses who have never even heard of Vatican II. Or, if they have heard of it, are unable to give a fair account of it. This is not their fault, of course. The Council made big headlines from 1962 through 1965, but that was twenty years or more before most of my students were born. Then, after the Council, religious educators moved away from the "catechism mentality" prevalent before Vatican II—which had focused on rote responses to a set of clear questions—to lead their students in a joyful Christianity of the heart. They taught their students to love God, and that simple quest overrode the need to ground them in a solid Catholic tradition.

We need to do both. We need to feel and we need to think. I believe it was St. Thomas Aquinas who reminded us that "virtue lies in the middle."

As a result of our recent efforts to make religion enjoyable, we see incoming freshmen who do not know the basic prayers or sacramental rituals of the faith. I had a student in one of my courses who was teaching religion in a local parish. One of her students only knew the "Hail Mary" as a famous desperation pass by Boston College's Doug Flutie in the closing seconds of the Orange Bowl Game in 1983. He knew about the Hail Mary pass, but he'd never heard about the Hail Mary prayer. Some students have never been to confession. One asked me if there was a priest in the confessional twenty-four hours a day. And another student told me she would go to the sacrament of reconciliation if she only knew the Act of Contrition.

This is not good. Given the current shortage of vocations in the church, I am convinced that the twenty-first-century church will need an informed laity that possesses theological vision (or at least some theological knowledge) that can be passed on to the next generation. And so I am writing this book for an audience I know well, my own students, and for college students everywhere. I am also thinking of potential Catholics (those in RCIA classes) and of lifelong Catholics as well—people in discussion groups, Catholic book circles, and parish groups of all kinds. These various groups are proliferating in surprising numbers because, apparently, people are still thirsting for the good news and looking for better ways to deliver it.

I have been meeting a good many of these people for the past eight years in my capacity as a national theological consultant to the William H. Sadlier Company, a publisher of Catholic textbooks. Sadlier has sent me to conferences and seminars all over the United States. These meetings are filled with intelligent Catholics, many of them religion teachers, catechists, liturgical ministers, pastoral associates, and parish leaders who are eager to know more about the process of growing up in the faith that we called Vatican II. And their questions, too, have helped me think more deeply about the implications of Vatican II—more deeply, but not I hope more abstrusely. I like to write simply, and I think that most people will understand the questions and answers that follow without going to a theological dictionary.

Think of this as a conversation that you might have walked in on during one of my classes, where the students laugh a lot and have fun trying to humor me. Or during one of my question and answer sessions at a Sadlier conference which, for all their light-heartedness, often deal in the ultimate questions—of life, death, and salvation—that puzzle us the most.

One

The Calling of Vatican II

1. What was Vatican II?

Shorthand for the Second Vatican Ecumenical Council, held in Rome in four sessions from October 1962 until December 1965. They called it the Second Vatican Council because it was a follow-up to the First Vatican Council, also held in Rome (though under completely different circumstances) a hundred years before. So these councils are fairly rare in the history of the church. They've only had twenty-one ecumenical councils, starting with the Council of Nicaea in 325 and the Council of Constantinople in 381. The church held two more ecumenical councils in the fifth century, the Council of Ephesus in 431, and the Council of Chalcedon in 451, one each in the sixth, seventh, eighth, and ninth centuries (Constantinople II in 553, Constantinople III in 680–681, Nicaea II in 787, Constantinople IV in 869–870). Seven papal councils occurred in the Middle Ages and are often referred to as "general" councils, followed by the Council of Constance in 1414–1418, the Council of Basel and Florence in the 1430s and 1440s, one in Rome in the early 1500s, and, probably the most well-known council before Vatican II, the Council of Trent, which met in stages from 1545–1563. More than three hundred years elapsed between Trent and Vatican I in 1869–1870.

2. What does *ecumenical* mean?

Ecumenical comes from a Greek word meaning *worldwide*. They've had other councils that were only local or regional affairs, like the Council of Arles in 314, or the three plenary councils of Baltimore during the early days of the U.S. church. According to Acts 15, Sts. Peter and Paul were involved in a kind of local council in Jerusalem, where they had a debate about what it meant to be a Christian and what it meant to be a Jew. Those early ecumenical councils at Nicaea and Constantinople convened delegates from "the whole world" that was known at the time. From our perspective in the twenty-first century, however, that "whole world" didn't extend farther than Asia Minor, what is now Greece and Turkey, and the Roman Empire. Vatican II was the first ecumenical council that brought in delegates from the whole globe.

3. In this context, what does *council* mean?

Ecumenical councils are not simply meetings. They have a legislative force. In fact, ecumenical councils—the pope and all the world's bishops acting together—enjoy the highest authority in the church. What an ecumenical council decides carries much more weight, for example, than a papal encyclical, or even canon law. (Canon law is only supposed to follow policies set by the pope or a council.) So councils are a kind of parliament of the world's bishops, headed by the Bishop of Rome, the pope. The church only arrived at this stage gradually, however. In the fifteenth century, the Council of Constance, which had delegates from the lower clergy as well as from the laity, ended up claiming that a council stood above the pope, in that it represented the whole church. Constance held that if a council was legitimately assembled in the Holy Spirit, it took its authority directly from Christ, and that all Christians, including the pope, had to obey it in matters of faith, the removal of schism, and the reform of the church. Constance seemed to mark a turning point for the church. It deposed two popes and forced the resignation of a third; all three were rival claimants to the papacy. And it also decreed that the church should hold frequent, regular councils as the best means of a lasting reform in the church.

Modern commentators, like the American Jesuit Francis Sullivan, agree with this notion. Sullivan has suggested the church get together in council every fifty years. In 1995, Pope John Paul II said in his encyclical *Ut Unum Sint* that even though the pope can define dogmas of faith without summoning a council (as the Fathers of Vatican I decreed), even this must be done "in communion with" his brother bishops. Pius IX and Pius XII consulted all the world's bishops by letter before they defined two Marian dogmas (the Immaculate Conception in 1854, and the Assumption in 1950), so that even these two "ex-cathedra, infallible" decisions were somewhat democratic because the pope didn't make them until he had asked all the world's bishops to take part in them.

Father Sullivan suggests that future popes could enlist the participation of his brother bishops without calling a council. He could invite them to discuss questions in their regional conferences, and then have them express their views and cast deliberative votes in a synod. Father Sullivan's rationale for such an approach is significant. He says that the decisions taken after such a wide consultation, even definitive statements on matters of faith and morals, would be "more convincing." The pope would not simply issue pronouncements from on high, but would seek a consensus from the whole church before any settlement concerning matters of faith and morals. Or, as Archbishop John Quinn urged in *The Reform of the Papacy,* a small but important book published in 1999, "What concerns all should be discussed and approved by all," which reasserted a principle dating back to the Roman Empire.

When the U.S. bishops prepared their two pastoral letters on peace and on the economy in the 1980s, they held public hearings, then published two drafts inviting general comments from lay people, and made extensive revisions in the light of those comments before publishing the letters. The church in the United States didn't invent this participative process. It was standard operating procedure in any of a number of American democratic institutions including the U.S. House of Representatives and the U.S. Senate. But that consultation employed by the U.S. bishops also came out of the spirit of Vatican II, which used a code word for this participative process. The Council Fathers called it collegiality. Some commentators on Vatican II said that if the church took a collegial approach to all of its decisions, it would begin to look more and more like a democracy.

4. But the church is not a democracy, is it?

The church has been governed in different ways through the centuries. For the first eight centuries, popes were elected by a vote of the people of Rome. That was a kind of democracy. The first bishop in U.S. history, John Carroll of Baltimore, was elected by a vote of all the priests in the thirteen colonies of the new republic. And even after the papacy took on much of the character of a feudal monarchy, ecumenical councils themselves were marked by furious, often heated debates, and lobbying, and voting, and majority rule. So ecumenical councils look very much like parliaments everywhere.

5. Who calls a council?

In modern times, the pope does. But the Roman Emperor Constantine proclaimed the Council of Nicaea in 325, and he took part in its deliberations. Pope John XXIII issued his first call for Vatican II at a private meeting he had with seventeen of his cardinals on January 25, 1959, shortly after he was elected pope. He was seventy-six when he was elected (upon the death of Pius XII) to be an interim pope, or simple caretaker. Then he went ahead and made one of the most radical moves taken by any pope, ever. John XXIII wanted the Council to renew the church according to the gospel (Hans Küng, *The Council in Action* [New York: Sheed and Ward, 1963], p. 75). No one challenged his assumption—that earlier Christianity was somehow more pure than later Christianity. But no one had to—no one, at least, who was familiar with the accretions of history that had made the medieval church and the Renaissance church and the modern church such a far cry from the simple church of the catacombs. The radical thing was that John XXIII believed the church ought to look at "the signs of the times," in order to meet the needs of the times. He used the Italian word *aggiornamento,* which means "a bringing up to date." It is a word that some said is dangerously close to Martin Luther's word *reform.* Other councils had been called to deal with specific heresies or crises in the church. Pope John could well have used the word *reform.* But he was too canny to frighten those who might oppose reform or, indeed, any radical changes at all. John XXIII said his council would be a pastoral council.

6. What is a pastoral council?

By contrast to many previous councils, like the Council of Nicaea in 325, the Council of Constantinople in 381, the Council of Ephesus in 431, the Council of Chalcedon in 451, Lateran IV in 1215, the Council of Constance in 1414–1418, and the Council of Trent that began in 1545, which were all called to deal with specific doctrinal issues that had put the church in crisis, Pope John's council took history itself as a starting point. In the hundred years since Vatican I, the world had changed in more ways than it had in the entire history of the church. In order to make the Christian message understandable in that vastly changed world, the church had to look for new ways of conveying that message. Pope John said he didn't want to change any of the articles of faith. He did want the Council Fathers to figure out new ways of getting the faith message across to the world. That's what the pope meant by a pastoral council.

7. What was the initial response to Pope John XXIII's announcement?

Genuine surprise, in fact, shocked silence on the part of the cardinals themselves, who had grown used to the notion that nothing needed changing. For many of them, the church was a perfect society. This thinking can be traced back to the First Vatican Council. The Church came to be understood as a hierarchical society in which some of the members are clergy and others are laity. The clergy received a divinely instituted power to teach and govern. The laity did not.

Steeped in that tradition, some cardinals believed that, once the pope's teaching authority was declared infallible at Vatican I, the (even now more imperial) church had no further need of councils. The pope, with God's help, could do everything the church needed, all by himself. But John XXIII believed that God's help (including that of the Holy Spirit) usually came through the mediation of others. In this case, he hoped it would come through the world's bishops.

8. So, then, everyone pitched in to prepare for the Council?

Not really. Some of the world's bishops grumbled. They noted that seminaries and convents were filled with candidates, Catholic schools were flourishing, and most Catholics had a very clear understanding of what being a Catholic entailed. How could a council make things any better? One American bishop remarked, "Why break up the Yankees?" Changes even then being proposed (like Mass in the vernacular) seemed to portend some danger for the church—or, possibly, to the elite status of the clergy. In his opening address to the Council, John XXIII called them "prophets of doom who are always forecasting disaster....In the present order of things, Divine Providence is leading us to a new order of human relations which...are directed toward the fulfillment of God's superior and inscrutable designs." Some helping to prepare the council agenda (mostly members of the pope's bureaucracy, the Roman Curia) didn't understand. The Curia first sent notes around the world, for instance, asking how the church ought to go about updating itself; they asked cardinals, bishops, priests, and the faculties of some thirty-seven Catholic universities to send in their ideas (called *postulata*), to be cast, naturally, in Latin. They also asked for *postulata* from superiors of male religious orders. (They did not approach the superiors heading religious orders of women.)

More than 2,000 *postulata* came in, but historians who have sifted through them say many of the requests were timid suggestions dealing with "bell, book and candle," that is, strictly churchy matters of little interest to most Catholics. There is no evidence that anyone asked for a change in the church's teaching on birth control, which all Catholics believed was unchangeable. In any event, the council's preparatory commissions, led by the heads of various Roman departments (called dicasteries), came up with drafts of some seventy documents (called *schemata*). Many of the seventy *schemata* simply repeated what had been taught by the church since the Council of Trent, and in the same kind of legalistic language. They were replete with stern condemnations of everything, from atheism to eroticism.

9. How long did the preparation period go on?

Preparations for the Council lasted almost four years. And, though some of the pope's advisors said they weren't ready, John XXIII wanted to get the Council started. He was thoroughly convinced that his call for a council was an inspiration of the Holy Spirit and that humankind was entering into a new phase of history. In other words, the Spirit was speaking to the church through "the signs of the times," that is, through history. That included contemporary history, which was part of "a hidden plan of Divine Providence." A verdict from Papa Roncalli's doctors that he was dying of cancer may have also been a sign that this was no time to tarry. If John XXIII didn't set things in motion immediately, there was no guarantee that his successor would pursue a council at all. He knew that Pius XII had planned a council after World War II. Those plans were derailed by cautious souls within the Roman Curia, and by the pope's own perfectionism. Pope John was quite content to let things happen. He might even have quoted G. K. Chesterton: "If a thing's worth doing, it's worth doing badly."

10. What did John XXIII mean by "the signs of the times"?

The expression came out of a new "theology of the world." The church's tie to the world was in keeping with an old idea: that the church was "incarnational," a community begun by the Word-made-flesh, by a God who chose to enter human history and start his pilgrim people on a march through that history. The word *incarnation* refers to the act of God becoming man, of God being made present in the world in a unique manner in the person of Jesus of Nazareth. Christian theology maintains that Jesus is the sacrament of God because sacraments make God present. When the risen Christ ascended to the Father, he instructed the new community of disciples to continue his saving activity. The Christian Church would make God present in the world. The Fathers of Vatican II would refer to the church as a sacrament, both a sign and a cause of grace, intended to lead the whole human race to salvation, not only in the next life, but in this life, too. "I am come that you may have life, and have it more abundantly," said Jesus, who was the sacrament of the Father, just as the church was to become the sacrament of the risen Christ. This sacramental activity continues throughout the history of the church.

At the Council, the bishops came to a corollary of this idea: that the church continues to grow through time, as its members, extensions of the living Christ, continue to deepen understandings of that mission. The Belgian Cardinal Leo Joseph Suenens was a strong advocate of this principle, recognizing that the church, the people of God, moves through history and is conditioned by history.

11. The church was supposed to change as the world changed?

Yes, but that wasn't as revolutionary an idea as it sounded at first. Church historians are telling us now that the church has been changing since the very beginning. At the time of Vatican II, the church had undergone very few changes since the Council of Trent in the sixteenth century, when the official church began to withdraw into a fortress mentality, a mentality especially prevalent in the eighteenth and nineteenth centuries. Pope John XXIII said the time had come to open the windows and let in some fresh air.

12. Did everyone agree with that metaphor, that the church had to open its windows and let in some fresh air?

No. There was an argument about it. Some who were called *conservatives* said the church needed no changes at all. Leaders of the church's liberal wing disagreed. They insisted that every living thing has to grow or die. But the pope's own words at the beginning of Vatican II carried the most weight. John XXIII said he didn't want the church to become a mausoleum—that the Fathers were to take "a leap forward" by making the gospel relevant to the people living on the planet today. He said, "For the substance of the ancient doctrine of the deposit of faith is one thing, and the way in which it is presented is another" (Pope John XXIII, "Opening Address," Second Vatican Council, Oct. 11, 1962). Some commentators believe this was the most important thing John XXIII ever uttered. With these words, he signaled that the time had come for the church to come down from the ramparts.

The popes of the eighteenth and nineteenth centuries had been battling the forces of the modern world, particularly that of the Enlightenment which led to the French Revolution of 1789, and all such secular movements toward democracy and freedom. Actually, the roots of this defensive fortress mentality began even earlier, in reaction to the Protestant Reformation and the devastating collapse of Christian unity. Somehow the church came to believe that the way to avoid such crises in the future would be to insulate itself behind a power structure that would claim to have all the answers.

This was an unfortunate premise because, as theological developments over the centuries have shown, the act of faith is primarily a surrender to the mystery. Theology helped us to recognize that the object of the human search is God, who is best defined as mystery. And this is not a mystery that humans have the tools to unravel. John XXIII appears to have understood this fact and, alongside this understanding, he had an optimistic view of the world because it was redeemed by Christ, a world in which the redemption was ongoing. This allowed him to say "yes" to this world and "yes" to history. He understood that if there was anything that marked the twentieth century, it was the passing on of power, from old elite institutions to the people. And he saw that passing as something good. For the people of God were growing up, moving beyond what might be termed a "catechism mentality," an approach to the faith that was based more on having all the right answers than on being taught how to raise the important questions.

Two

The Players, the Tensions, the Media

13. Who attended Vatican II?

At the beginning of October 1962, more than twenty-two hundred cardinals, archbishops, bishops and abbots (and several hundred theologians, called *periti*) streamed into Rome, more than a thousand from Europe, almost five hundred from Latin America, four hundred from North America, almost four hundred from Asia, almost three hundred from Africa. They came on jets. They came on trains. They came on buses. One bishop from Africa even hitchhiked to Naples on a tramp steamer, then bought a second-class train ticket to Rome.

Vatican II brought the church to the threshold of the new millennium. At the beginning of the last Council, Vatican I, in 1869, there were 737 Council Fathers in attendance, most of them from Europe. Now, in 1962, for the first time, the church was seen as a truly world church, multicultural and catholic in the fullest sense of the word.

The world press also noticed the presence of some figures who were new to ecumenical councils of the past thousand years: official observers from the Orthodox world, and from the mainline Christian churches, such as Lutherans, Episcopalians and Anglicans, Methodists, Presbyterians, and Quakers. There were even some Jewish observers. This was a revolutionary move.

14. What was so revolutionary about it?

After 1054, Catholics and Orthodox kept talking to each other—mostly quarreling and fighting—but negotiations were on and off. As recently as Vatican I, Protestants were viewed in a very negative light. One of the best bishop-theologians at Vatican I, Archbishop Josef Strossmayer of Bosnia-Herzogovina, was severely criticized when he had some good things to say about

Protestants. Some shouted at him that he was a heretic. In Vatican II, we saw something completely different. As Robert McAfee Brown, one of the observers, noted: "We used to be called schismatics and heretics. Now we are called 'separated brethren.'" Jewish observers at Vatican II were not always treated so kindly. Some bishops from Arab countries in the Middle East grumbled openly about the presence of the Jews, and their being right up in the choicest box seats at the front of the conciliar hall. But this was a spill-over from political battles then being fought (and still being fought) in the Middle East; it had nothing to do with the main reason for the Jewish presence at the Council. There was an item on the conciliar agenda placed there by Cardinal Augustine Bea that was intended to exonerate Jews from the age-old charge that the Jewish people had to pay forever for killing Christ, a position justified by some based on Matthew 27:25: "His blood be upon us and on our children."

15. Who was Cardinal Bea?

He was the president of the Secretariat for Promoting Christian Unity, and one of the key figures at the Council pushing for Christian unity. One of the major things he had to contend with: old attitudes, even among some of his admirers, who kept talking about Christian unity in terms of "a return to the church" on the part of the Orthodox and the Lutherans. "We are not talking about *un ritorno,*" he told a reporter, thumbing an article in *l'Osservatore Romano,* the official Vatican daily, that kept using the word *ritorno.* "Members of other Christian churches who are living today never 'left' the church. So they cannot 'return,' can they? We are talking about going together, hand in hand, toward a new future."

Bea was a lean, almost cadaverous German Jesuit and a scriptural scholar by trade who had lived in Rome for decades as rector of the Pontifical Biblical Institute. John XXIII put him in charge of all the church's outreach to other Christian bodies (and the Jews) at Vatican II, but he drew consistent and powerful opposition from Cardinal Alfredo Ottaviani.

16. Who was Cardinal Ottaviani?

He was the prefect of the Holy Office, formerly known as the Holy Office of the Inquisition, and he headed a faction at the Council that wanted no radical changes. In fact, Cardinal Ottaviani (whose coat of arms was inscribed with the words *Semper Idem,* "always the same") opposed bringing observers to the Council. In 1960, he tried to block a move by Cardinal Bea to send the Jesuit Jean Danielou to the World Council of Churches' meeting in New Delhi on the grounds that this would only trigger expectations from Protestants and Orthodox that they would be invited to Vatican II. Ottaviani finally relented. He stipulated that Danielou could go to New Delhi, but he would have to stay away from Vatican II. Danielou went to New Delhi, but nothing could prevent him from coming to Rome for the Council. He came, not only as a private *peritus* for the French bishops, but he also served as a daily briefing officer for the French-speaking press. And, of course, the Protestant and Orthodox observers were given places of honor inside the conciliar hall (that was Pope John's idea) as men from Cardinal Bea's secretariat whispered translations of the Latin interventions into their ears.

17. What's an intervention?

Intervention was just a translation of the Italian word *intervento,* which meant, in this context, "a speech." All the interventions were in Latin, which were difficult for many of the Council Fathers to follow. (The Fathers said they needed simultaneous translators, too, but that never happened.) Some of the bishops asked the Council's secretary-general, Pericle Felici, to publish transcripts of each day's proceedings, as the *Congressional Record* does for the U.S. Congress. But that didn't happen either, much to the consternation of some bishops who didn't handle

Latin very well. Some of the Fathers even had a hard time delivering the speeches that had been ghosted for them. Cardinal Spellman of New York had someone else deliver his interventions. One of the Council's most colorful and truculent characters, the Melkite Patriarch Maximos IV Saigh, from Beirut, came up with his own singular solution. He always spoke in French.

18. Where did everyone live? And who paid for their stay in Rome?

Those bishops who could afford it were scattered in some of Rome's best hotels. Many of the U.S. bishops settled into the Rome Hilton. Some of them treated themselves (and their clerical aides) to rooms at the exclusive hotels on the Via Veneto. Cardinal Spellman of New York had a suite at Rome's grandest hotel (named, of course, the Grand Hotel). Some bishops stayed in cheap *pensioni.* If a bishop from a poor nation could not afford even modest lodgings, the Vatican paid for him and, in some cases, for his travel, too. Many other bishops stayed in the simple rooms provided for them at their national residential colleges in Rome—the Brazilian College, the English College, the Spanish College, and so on. Bishops from religious orders, like the Jesuits, the Franciscans, and the Dominicans, were welcome in their own international headquarters. Some two dozen bishops from the missionary Society of the Divine Word stayed at their generalate south of Rome. Bishop Ernest Primeau of Manchester, New Hampshire, took modest lodging in the Villanova, along with some of the Council's theologians, including John Courtney Murray, S.J., where they had rollicking discussions every night about what had transpired at the Council earlier in the day. The retired Jesuit archbishop of Bombay, T. D. Roberts, was a houseguest of *Time* magazine's man at the Council. The Canadian bishops, residing together at the Canadian College, turned their togetherness into a decided advantage: several nights a week they invited the best scholars in the church to come and brief them in a series of theological seminars.

19. Why did the bishops feel the need for theological seminars?

Because, in some of the church's best institutions of higher learning there had been a tremendous outburst of theological, historical, and scriptural research for the past twenty years (roughly since the end of World War II). Many of those who had done the best scholarship in these fields were also in Rome for the Council as experts, and they helped many of the bishops go way beyond what they had learned during their seminary days—often from textbooks that had not been updated much since the Council of Trent in 1563. At one point during the Council's first session, Cardinal Ottaviani tried to forbid lectures to the bishops by Jesuits from the Biblical Institute in Rome. He even asked the pope to banish Jesuit theologian Karl Rahner from Rome. The pope refused. Unfazed, Ottaviani issued an order that the *periti* should not approach a bishop unless they were asked for advice.

Most of the bishops were grateful to the *periti* for their help. Denis Hurley, the archbishop of Durban, South Africa, said this was an example of the Holy Spirit at work. Many of these *periti,* Hurley noted, had been squelched in the years before the Council. "Now, the bishops were sitting at *their* feet hearing what they had to say. It was a wonderful experience, organized by the bishops' conferences, a kind of university education on the cheap" ("Pioneer and Prophetic Voice: Archbishop Denis Hurley of Durban," in *Renewal: Newsletter of the Cardinal Suenens Center* [vol. 1, no. 1]: p. 4).

Indeed, the *periti* themselves were the principal writers and editors of the projects the bishops were voting on, an all-star cast of theologians whose like the church may have never seen in one place before: Karl Rahner, Edward Schillebeeckx, M. D. Chenu, Yves Congar, Henri de Lubac, Jean Danielou, John Courtney Murray, and Gerard Phillips, a man who worked long, killing hours rewriting the texts in accord with the suggestions and amendments (called *adnexa*) that poured in by the thousands from the Council Fathers. Most of the Council Fathers were grateful for the help given by the *periti.* Some were not so grateful. One day, Archbishop John Carmel Heenan of Westminster in London recalled the Greek gift of a wooden horse at Troy, and told the Council Fathers, "I fear the Greeks, bearing gifts."

20. Was the world press at the Council in force?

Not really. Not at first. Few in the world press really understood what was happening at Vatican II, or why anyone but church professionals should be interested in it. Early press accounts were poorly informed, in part because those who were running the Council wouldn't let reporters inside the Council (as they were customarily allowed into every parliamentary proceeding in the free world). The rules of the Council, written by the Roman Curia, banned the press from St. Peter's (although a few journalists were admitted each day for the Mass that began the proceedings and then ushered out). Furthermore, the rules said that the Council was to be conducted in strict secrecy.

This was ironic. One of the Council's original seventy *schemata* dealt with the mass media as a potential instrument of the church's outreach, but the Roman Curia seemed determined to keep everything at the Council under wraps. Early briefings by something that was called the Vatican Press Office were anything but helpful. In his first meeting with reporters, the Council's press spokesman, Fausto Vaillanc, ticked off the names of Council Fathers who spoke that day, but he didn't reveal what they said. Even the draft documents written in Latin were labeled *sub secreto.*

21. Why the official secrecy at the Council?

According to a long-time Vatican watcher, the American journalist Robert Blair Kaiser, "opening up the Council to the press would have implied that the Council Fathers were accountable to the people, which, to members of the Roman Curia, would amount to an attenuation of the church's 'sovereignty.'" Kaiser says that insistence on sovereignty "is still in evidence in the twenty-first century Vatican. Members of the Curia still bring it up whenever there is a call for opening up the secret meetings of synods and consistories" (Robert Blair Kaiser, "Secret Disservice," in *U.S. Catholic,* May 2002, pp. 41–42). Cardinal Jan Schotte, who has run the synods in Rome since 1982, and was in charge of the Extraordinary Consistory of Cardinals in May 2001, told members of the Vatican Press Corps on June 1, 2001: "The bishops are accountable only to the pope. And the pope is only accountable to God."

Some critics of the Roman Curia say the Curia is unfriendly to any and every change in the church, because the church is, to them, unchangeable. That is an exaggeration. In many ways, the Curia is very up-to-date. It has taken many cues from the Fathers of Vatican II, who took Pope John's call for *aggiornamento* seriously by calling for changes that would help them proclaim, witness, and serve the gospel in a radically new kind of world. But many members of the Curia were rather retro at the beginning of Vatican II, and their views were reflected in the press. Arnaldo Cortesi, Rome correspondent for the *New York Times,* may have listened too exclusively to these cautious voices inside the Vatican. Just before the Council began, he advised readers of the *Times* not to expect any radical changes at Vatican II. But on the Council's first working day, the Fathers revolted.

22. There was a revolt on the Council's first day?

On October 13, 1962, much to everyone's surprise, the very senior French Cardinal Achille Liénart took the microphone to object that the Fathers were being asked to vote for a preselected slate of company men (that is, mostly members of the Roman Curia) on each of ten conciliar commissions charged with managing the conciliar agenda. Liénart suggested the Fathers might want to make their own lists. The German Cardinal Josef Frings seconded his call, and both cardinals got resounding applause from the twenty-two hundred Fathers assembled in the bleachers that had been erected inside the nave of St. Peter's.

The Council moderators promptly adjourned the meeting, and gave the Fathers a week to come up with their own lists. When the voting was over, many of the company men had been replaced by the nominees of the leading language-groups at the council: the French, the Germans, the Dutch, and the Belgians. The Netherlands and Belgium had less than two dozen bishops at the Council from their dioceses, but those analyzing a list of the Council Fathers found there were no less than a hundred Dutch and Belgian bishops on the list from Asia, Africa, and Latin America. These missionary bishops tended to gravitate toward their confreres at home, who were led by two of the most progressive cardinals at the Council, the Dutchman Jan Alfrink, and the Belgian Leo Josef Suenens.

A Dutch bishop from Tanganyika, Josef Blomjous, was elected president of all the bishops of Africa, who (it soon became clear) had voted with the majority in revolt against the Roman Curia. The revolt prompted one insider to claim, "This really is a council."

In 1985, Cardinal Joseph Ratzinger tried to rewrite this early history of the Council by maintaining that Pope John XXIII was angry when the Council Fathers revolted. But in an interview I had in Sotto il Monte with Pope John's long-time secretary, Loris Capovilla, in January 2001, Capovilla (by now a bishop) assured me that Pope John was delighted that the Fathers were asserting themselves. Michael Walsh, another conciliar historian, said this move demonstrated "the council was in charge of its own proceedings." Being "in charge" meant they could rewrite the *schemata* that had been fashioned by proponents of an ecclesiology that was firmly founded on the kind of thinking that emerged from the Council of Trent.

23. What was wrong with the Council of Trent?

As the Fathers of Vatican II would soon point out, Trent, which was called in response to the Protestant Reformation, produced a systematic theology calculated to defend the church against reformers like Martin Luther. That theology was legalistic, and the church that came out of it put a high premium on the power of an authority that started with the pope at the top of an ecclesiastic pyramid. That ecclesiology stressed the letter of the law rather than the spirit of the gospel, and it had ramifications in many areas. I cite here only one of them, the field of moral theology. Many in the church that predated Vatican II followed a largely negative "rule-book Catholicism." For example, if we ate meat on a Friday, that was a mortal sin; dying unrepentant, we would go to hell.

It didn't take the bishops at Vatican II very long to correct that notion. There was no conciliar decree on this; the bishops of the United States, for example, just exercised their common sense by coming home and telling folks the church could not make something a mortal sin that was not sinful in itself. They revoked the "no meat on Friday rule," and only winced a little when they saw a cartoon in *The New Yorker* that had an assistant devil asking his chief, in hell, "What do we do with all the guys who ate meat on Friday?"

All of a sudden, average Catholics had a new, more radical take on sin. Sin wasn't about eating meat on Friday. Sin was putting God out of their lives completely. Many Catholics stopped going to confession, but the surprising, delightful thing was that at communion time, practically everyone was marching up to receive. This was one way the people at large started reacting in concert with the reformers of Vatican II, who were downplaying the old rulebook mentality and trying to take the church back to its more concrete sources in the primitive church, where early Christians rejoiced in the message of Jesus: that he had come that they might have life and have it more abundantly.

Three

First Session: October 11–December 8, 1962

Giving the Church Back to the People

Returning to the Church's Primitive Beginnings

24. So, how did the conciliar debate finally begin?

It began with a debate on the liturgy. John XXIII himself decided to put the liturgy first for two reasons: (1) It was the one *schema* that had been fashioned by those interested in his kind of reform, that is, an attempt to cut away some historical accretions and go back to a more primitive, more pure Christianity, and (2) it dealt with a subject that would have the most impact on the people at large—the Mass. According to an old adage in the church, what the people believe follows as a consequence of how they pray: *Lex orandi est lex credendi.*

In fact *Sacrosanctum Concilium,* the Constitution on Sacred Liturgy, was the first completed document at the Council, promulgated on December 4, 1963. A vigorous liturgical movement that had been going on for more than a century before, primarily in Europe, was one reason for this topic to be dealt with so early. There was also evidence of a good deal of interest in the United States dating back to the 1920s and 1930s. Another reason for the early promulgation of this document was, as Pope Paul VI noted, the liturgy's "intrinsic worth and importance for the life of the Church." The liturgy touches all the members directly. The opening lines of the Constitution attest to this fact: "It is the goal of this most sacred Council to intensify the daily growth of Catholics in Christian living...to nurture whatever can contribute to the unity of all who believe in Christ....The Council has special reasons for judging it a duty to provide for the renewal and fostering of the liturgy."

25. The conservatives wanted to keep the Mass in Latin, and the progressives wanted it to be in the vernacular?

This was going to be a pastoral council, with a huge emphasis on serving the people, the millions of Catholics around the world. Edward Schillebeeckx said Vatican II "broke the clergy's monopoly of the liturgy." He explained: "Whereas it was formerly the priest's affair, with the faithful no more than his clientele, the Council regards not only the priest but the entire Christian community, God's people, as the subject of the liturgical celebration." And it followed, he said, that if the people were doing the liturgy, they should be doing it in their own language (Eduard Schillebeechx, The Real Achievement of Vatican II, trans. H. J. J. Vaughan [London: Herder and Herder, 1967], pp. 27–28).

After a furious and protracted debate, the Council ruptured almost two thousand years of history, in the Western Roman church at least, by proposing that the Mass could be in the vernacular. Since the discussion on liturgy had been so heated, and since a good number of the Fathers had expressed rather negative opinions of the *schema,* this vote, the Council's first, was awaited with a great deal of tension. The vote took place on November 14. There was enormous surprise when the *schema* was approved by 2,162 of the Fathers out of a possible total of 2,215. Only forty-six Fathers voted against the *schema* (seven votes were invalid). One of those opposed to the vernacular—the cardinal archbishop of Los Angeles, James Francis McIntyre—couldn't speak Latin, and hardly understood it. Confused during the vote, he cast his ballot for the vernacular, and walked away from the conciliar hall that day, dusting his hands and telling a colleague, "Well, I guess we fixed those liturgists today."

26. Why the big argument about language?

It seemed very elementary to us pragmatic Americans: what was intended by and for the people should be understood by the people. Beneath the talk about language, however, the Council Fathers were speaking the grammar of power, and about the inadvisability of handing it over to the people.

The word *vernacular* has a larger meaning of both philosophical and sociological importance. It is a concept that can also stand for whatever is homebred, homespun, homegrown, and homemade. By contrast, Latin is the language of the elite. (It is worth noting here that Latin *had been* the vernacular at one time, but not for at least fifteen hundred years.) And this elitism was one reason why the traditionalists at the Council were so opposed to the vernacular. Especially since the Council of Trent (which ran from 1545 to 1563), the Curia had been engaged in a centralizing and expropriating control—and it was a process that had only become the order of the day under Pius IX and the twentieth-century popes. Allowing the church's worship in the vernacular would reverse that centralizing process, not only of worship, but of power in many other areas as well. When Cardinal Ottaviani, and others in the traditionalist minority, resisted the vernacular, they were implicitly resisting a shift of power in the church—power to the people. But they were outnumbered, much to everyone's surprise—outvoted ten to one, in fact, by the pastoral-minded bishops from Panama to Nagpur who knew they were there to serve the people.

27. So the progressives won the first battle of the Council?

I'd say the people won. The Fathers of Vatican II took away one of the last vestiges of the sacramental divide between the ordained and the nonordained when they approved taking communion in the hand, and giving the laity the cup as well. Some Fathers argued against that on the grounds that women would leave their lipstick on the chalice! The American theologian Joseph Komonchak observed, "I did not count that as one of the most serious issues." Clearly, this was not the Council's finest hour.

28. What was the Council's finest hour?

Well, in the first session at least, it was probably a speech given during a preliminary debate on the *schema De Ecclesia* (On the Church) by Bishop Emile Joseph DeSmedt of Bruges, Belgium. He urged that the church leave behind its juridicism, its clericalism, and its triumphalism. For his impassioned eloquence, he received the loudest and most sustained applause of the entire Council. In one of the most interesting accounts of this debate, Xavier Rynne (a pseudonym for Fr. Francis X. Murphy, a Redemptorist Father present as an observer at the Council) wrote at length, and rather colorfully, about DeSmedt's speech. DeSmedt said that all forms of "triumphalism" should be avoided when talking about the church. He was referring to a pompous and overbearing attitude that had little relation, he said, to the message of the New Testament. He claimed that "clericalism" was equally offensive and that the church is not a pyramid of pope, bishops, priests, nuns, and finally the laity; rather, the church is the people of God. And instead of a juridical mentality, quite prevalent in the days before the Council, DeSmedt claimed that the church should be placed before the world as the mother of humankind. Clearly DeSmedt's words would set the tone for many of the Council debates.

29. Kind of surprising, isn't it, to have a group of clerics applauding someone who was calling for an end to clericalism?

I think the Council Fathers were trying to give the church back to the people. One of the many ways they tried to do that was by urging first-class citizenship for the laity, which would explain why they placed the people of God in chapter one of *Lumen Gentium,* the Dogmatic Constitution on the Church. In a way, they were fashioning a much more democratic definition of the church. The church was not the pope, or the pope and the bishops. It was "the people of God." The real significance of this change didn't dawn on many reporters until much later: the fact that lay people were being invited not only to assume full membership in the church, but to grow up in the faith as well.

30. How did the Council help update the church's theology?

First, by going back to one of the principal sources of the faith: the Bible itself. For almost the whole twentieth century, modern Catholic scholars had been attempting to work on the

Bible's meaning, which was fairly obscure to their contemporaries because it was written by persons from ancient cultures for people of their own time and place. But these scholars believed they had a duty to discover what God was saying to those peoples and, by extension, to the people of the twentieth century.

At the Council, however, reactionary forces from the Roman Curia tried to yank the scholars' licenses that had been given them, in effect, by Pope Pius XII in his encyclical *Divino Afflante Spiritu*. Father Augustine Bea, S.J., was the rumored ghost writer of that encyclical. Now, as Cardinal Bea, he had to defend it here at Vatican II, under the attack of some self-styled "defenders of the faith." Those defenders wrote a draft document, "Schema Constitutionis dogmaticae de Fontibus Revelationis," "On the Twin Sources of Revelation," that would have closed down all Catholic biblical scholarship. They believed that "making sense out of Scripture" was tantamount to saying it wasn't true. The Council Fathers spurned the reactionaries and voted for the scholars. They did so because they had faith that real scholarship would serve the increasingly well-educated people of God with what they needed. They could understand the real meanings in Scripture and not just swallow words they couldn't understand. The practical effect of the conciliar decree on Scripture was this: Catholic theologians would be allowed to exercise their interpretive talents over scriptural texts. In fact, they had a duty to do so. In effect, the Council was suggesting "rich possibilities for theological innovation"—which was the only way that Catholic scholars could help push the enlistment of the people of God in contemporary causes that would have been unthinkable in pre-conciliar Catholicism. Casting the vote they did would also help contribute to the church's new ecumenical thrust.

31. What do you mean by "ecumenical thrust"?

"Ecumenical" not only means "worldwide" (as in "ecumenical council"), but it also refers to the modern move toward the unity of all Christians, which was a principal reason why John

XXIII called a council in the first place. But this goal of John XXIII's for Christian unity would be in stark contrast to the pre-Vatican II official mindset, one that was not interested in ecumenism. This approach to Christian unity was clear: the only way to foster Christian unity was to promote the return to the one true church of Christ by those who had left it. And Catholics at the time viewed members of other Christian churches as misguided people. Before the Council, Catholics were ordered to stay away from Protestants. Many U.S. Catholics were told that if they went to a Protestant wedding they would incur automatic excommunication, and were even warned against sending their children to a Protestant summer camp.

32. How did the Council promote Christian unity?

The Council did that in a number of ways. One was by taking the church back to its more primitive beginnings, before the great schism between East and West in the eleventh century, and before the Protestant revolt in the sixteenth century. Putting the Mass in the vernacular (which Martin Luther had done four centuries before) was one way. Making the church's theology more biblical (another contribution made by Luther) was another way. One of the most startling developments was *Nostra Aetate,* the Declaration on the Relation of the Church to Non-Christian Religions, which for the first time acknowledged the truth and holiness in other religions as the work of the one living God. (This document was promulgated during the fourth session of the Council, but deserves mention here because of its significance in the area of Christian unity.) Yet another way, seen clearly toward the end of the Council's first session, was the beginning of the redefining of papal primacy—a great obstacle to Christian unity, particularly with the Orthodox. The Council Fathers also attempted to "complete" Vatican I, with a reconsideration of the relationship between the primacy of the pope and the office of the bishops.

33. What does *primacy* mean?

The pope is the bishop of Rome and Catholicism has come to identify the pope with the role of Peter in the New Testament, in that he enjoyed a certain preeminence among the apostles. However, Catholics and other Christians disagree about the meaning and implications of Peter's role in the New Testament Church and, therefore, about the function of the papacy. Ecclesiologist Richard McBrien points to three areas of disagreement. Historically Catholics have held that Peter's leadership was conferred by Jesus himself, and that this special leadership is passed down to the successors of Peter, the popes. Non-Catholic Christians reject this notion of a succession in pastoral authority from Peter to the bishops of Rome. Theologically Catholics believe that the papacy is of divine law, while non-Catholics insist it is of human origin only. And, canonically, coming from Vatican I, Catholics see the legal power of the pope as supreme, full, and not subject to any higher human jurisdiction, while other Christians view such claims as tyranny waiting to happen.

34. Did Vatican II really succeed in redefining papal primacy?

No. The conciliar majority tried to say that the early church was founded on the twelve apostles (and not only Peter) and that the bishops who succeed them in time are not "working for the pope," but are vicars of Christ in their own churches. Especially helpful here is Chapter III in *Lumen Gentium,* the Dogmatic Constitution on the Church, where the bishops together are seen to constitute a stable body, or "college," which is collectively responsible for the needs of the entire church. And to avoid any misunderstanding, the principle of "collegiality" is explained in more precise language in a "Prefatory Note" to Chapter III that was prepared by the Theological Commission. It states: "In every instance it is clear that *the union* of the bishops *with their head* is contemplated, and never any action of the bishops taken *independently* of the Pope...this hierarchical communion of all the bishops with the Supreme

Pontiff is undoubtedly a recurring feature of tradition." This was progress. But the Council ended up taking some of the pope's power away with one hand and giving it back to him with the other. A good example of this "giving back" is the explanatory note that the drafters of *Lumen Gentium* added to assuage those Council Fathers who were extremely fearful of any undermining of papal primacy. As theologian Richard McBrien has noted, the Council majority was extremely displeased by this addition that stated: "As supreme pastor of the Church, the Sovereign Pontiff can always exercise his authority as he chooses, as is demanded by his office itself."

As a result, primacy is still an issue in many ecumenical dialogues. In 1995, Pope John Paul II was still calling for help here, even from Christians who were not Catholics, to see if they could come up with a redefinition that everyone could live with. And primacy continues to be a concern within the Catholic Church itself, in that many bishops believe that collegiality, as proposed by Vatican II, has yet to be implemented.

Four

A New Pope for the Second Session: September 29—December 4, 1963

The Pace Slows...Disagreements over Power Issues

35. Pope John XXIII died before his Council ended?

Yes, he was only around for the first session. In the winter and spring of 1963, during the waning days of his papacy, he made some significant moves to stop the Cold War. Then he died on June 3. After his death, the response from all over the world was unprecedented. Perhaps the statement from then Secretary-General to the United Nations, U Thant, best represents this overwhelming response: "A most noble life has come to an end...the death of Pope John XXIII was deeply felt by everyone who saw in him a symbol of universality, peace and harmony....In identifying himself so unreservedly with the cause of peace and international understanding, Pope John XXIII became the very embodiment of humankind's own aspirations in this uncertain period in history" (quoted in Richard Cardinal Cushing, *Call Me John* [Boston: Daughters of St. Paul, 1963], pp. 127–28). Another observer at the Council, Frederick Franck, called John XXIII "the manifestation of the Spirit in our time." No Christian could ever hope for a better tribute. Then came the conclave of 1963.

36. What's a conclave?

The word comes from the Italian phrase *con clave,* "with a key." It refers to the practice (begun in the thirteenth century) of locking the cardinals up while they are in the process of electing a new pope. Those in charge of the election did this (and still do it) mainly to keep the cardinals free from outside influences. In ancient times, the outside influences were often the noble families of Rome, vying to get their own men elected. Later, the crowned heads of Europe and power-mad leaders like Napoleon tried to have their way with the electors. In 1996, when Pope John Paul II tightened up the conclave, he seemed most concerned about keeping the mass media out. In his bull, *Universi Domenici Gregis,* he specified that no newspapers, radios, or televisions be allowed in the Casa Santa Marta, where the cardinals would be living while they were electing his successor.

37. What happened inside the conclave that elected John XXIII's successor?

It was common knowledge that Pope John XXIII believed that the conclave following his death would elect Cardinal Giovanni Battista Montini from Milan. John also believed that Montini would continue the Council, much to the dismay of some curial cardinals who had never been in favor of Vatican II. Other factors in Cardinal Montini's favor were his remarkable knowledge of the church and his clear commitment to continue the work of the Council. This conclave would be the largest conclave ever. Pope John had been elected in 1958 by fifty-one cardinals. In 1963, eighty-one cardinals were eligible to vote. Pope John died on June 3 and the conclave opened on June 17. After a good deal of political maneuvering, Cardinal Montini was elected on June 21. He chose to be called Paul VI and, in his very first address as pope, Paul VI declared that his pontificate would be devoted to the Council.

38. What was different about the Council when it resumed in 1963?

Now the press, sensing a bigger story, came to Rome in full force, and with heavier-hitting reporters. Prior to the first session, some 900 accreditation cards had been issued to journalists by the Press Office. By the end of the first session, the number rose to 1,255. The secrecy of the Council was beginning to shatter. From then on, permission was granted to reveal what was said in Council debates, though the Commission discussions would still be kept secret. The opening ceremony on September 19 was different as well. As noted in volume III of the scholarly *History of Vatican II* (Vol. III is edited by Giuseppe Alberigo and Joseph A. Komonchak [Maryknoll: Orbis, 2000].), while the opening ceremony of session one seemed marked by a triumphalistic and hierarchical mood, the ceremony marking the beginning of session two evidenced a mood of disenchantment. In his opening address, Pope Paul VI focused on the need for dialogue. One well-known commentator, Xavier Rynne, saw Paul VI's address as a bridge of continuity between the "Johannine" Council and the "Pauline" Council. Then, with the ceremony behind them, it was time to resume the business of the Council. Discussion on the *schema* on the church would be the first order of business and the contending forces were getting feistier, as the debate intensified over collegiality.

39. What's collegiality?

This term has been referred to earlier. But some additional comment is needed here because the idea played such a central role in the discussions on the church during this session. Some, oversimplifying the term, call it "democracy in the church." It is not quite that. But collegiality does refer to a kind of sharing of authority between Rome and all the other local churches. Each bishop represents his own local church, and the pope represents the local church of Rome which, by tradition, exercises a primacy of love over all the other local churches and has become the church-of-last-resort in disputed questions. By ordination, bishops become members of the college of bishops and thereby assume responsibility not only for their own dioceses but for the whole church. So, collegiality is the structural expression of the church-as-community. The early days of the second session witnessed crucial debates on collegiality and by the end of October, the terms *Vatican II* and *collegiality* would be inextricably linked. However, even after so many years, the issue of collegiality continues to be a sticking point in the church. Clearly, the debate still rages. One of the central points raised in contemporary commentaries on this issue points to the continued resistance of the Roman Curia to the implementation of collegiality.

40. What was it about the Roman Curia that needed reforming?

The papal offices in Rome were called the Curia since the eleventh century. The present structure was established in the sixteenth century (Congregations, Offices, Courts). Pius X made his own contribution—as did many others—in the early twentieth century. But, over the years, this group came to assume more authority and control over church matters, often creating tensions between the pope and his brother bishops. Their desire for control was very evident both during the preparatory phase of the Council and during the Council's actual deliberations. From the very beginning, the Curia sensed the threat that the Council might pose for them and even used every means available to prevent the Council from being held. Once they failed at stopping the Council, their efforts turned to tactics that would minimize any success the Council might have in renewing and reforming the church.

41. How did the conservatives fight back at the Council's second session?

Cardinal Ottaviani tried the politics of delay. Debate on the *schema De Ecclesia* (On the Church) went on for a month but Cardinal Ottaviani's Theological Commission refused to approve revisions of the text, based on amendments offered by the bishops. For much of the session, the Theological Commission (which was very much like the Rules Committee in the U.S. Congress) was only meeting once a week. It began to dawn on the Council's majority that Cardinal Ottaviani could get his way simply by stalling. To speed things up, Cardinal Suenens tried to call for a poll of the Fathers to move things along. The Council's secretary general, Pericle Felici, threatened to resign, and the pope himself had to take a hand by endorsing Suenens' call for a vote.

The Fathers voted, on October 30, to bring Ottaviani to heel, but Ottaviani was stubborn. He let it be known that his Theological Commission would regard such votes as guidelines, not directives. There was another showdown on November 8, during a discussion of the next *schema* on the pastoral office of bishops, which dealt with the interrelationship of pope, bishops, and the Roman Curia. Cardinal Frings of Cologne, assisted by a young *peritus* named Joseph Ratzinger, took the occasion on November 8 to remind the Theological Commission that it was there to carry out the wishes of the Council, not to tell the Council what it could or could not decide. Frings went on to criticize the Holy Office itself for its recent Star Chamber proceedings that ended up condemning theologians without due process.

Cardinal Ottaviani seized the microphone to lash back at Frings. He reasserted the authority of the Theological Commission over the Council, and claimed that an attack on the Holy Office was an attack on the pope himself as its prefect. But that very afternoon, Paul VI spoke with Frings to support him, and with Ottaviani, to say he was wrong.

There was another battle inside the Theological Commission, this time over the *schema* on ecumenism, most particularly over a chapter in it on religious liberty. Ottaviani tried to block any discussion on it and, when that failed, to delay referring the text to the Council. But, on November 12, he was outvoted in his own commission, and the document was sent to the printer.

On November 15, the pope intervened again, to side with the conciliar majority on the role of Ottaviani's commission which, the majority claimed, had no mandate to decide disputed issues, but simply to distill suggested amendments and put them to a vote of all the Council Fathers. On November 21, the pope decided to add six new members to all the commissions, and he said they should be chosen by a popular vote of the Council Fathers. Those votes brought more representatives of the majority to each commission, and shifted control of the Council even more dramatically to the side of reform.

The second session ended on December 3, but many were discouraged, including Pope Paul VI, because so little was actually nailed down. The pope, who had hoped to finish the Council in this second session, had to settle for a promise of more action at the third session, scheduled for the fall of 1964. The pope hoped that, after the Fathers finished *De Ecclesia* (which largely dealt with the church's internal governance), they would turn to another *schema* on the church in its relationship to the world.

Now the world press got even more interested in the Council. It was now clear that the Council was going to deal with issues that had a more direct impact on Catholics at large—Catholics who were not as interested in intramural church politics as they were about their own role in the world as followers of Jesus.

Five

Third Session: September 14–November 21, 1964

Working for Peace among the World's Religions

Rethinking the Ends of Marriage

42. What kicked off the debates at the Council's third session?

The bishops returned to the Council on September 14, 1964, finished their discussions on *De Ecclesia,* and then turned to a draft of a declaration on religious liberty. The conservative Cardinal Ruffini (from Palermo in Sicily) promptly attacked the concept of religious liberty. "We should call it 'religious tolerance,'" he said. "We cannot make a theological justification for religious liberty." He was harking back to the old notion that "error has no rights."

They had a small debate over what was called the *schema* on the Jews, which was intended by its sponsors in Cardinal Bea's office to remove the spurious biblical and theological underpinnings for an anti-Semitism that had marred the church's witness for centuries.

Then they took up the *schema* on ecumenism, which was the Council's way of dealing with a problem as compelling then as it was during the religious wars of an earlier age: establishing peace among the world's religions. How could any religion maintain its credibility if it fostered hatred and violence? Yet history was replete with tales of "religious" wars. The Council Fathers seemed especially anxious to correct the church's own stance toward other Christian churches. In their discussions concerning the *schema* on ecumenism, we heard many a bishop declare that the Body of Christ is not limited to the Roman Catholic Church, and that everyone who is baptized belongs to that Body of Christ. We also heard the bishops affirming the goodness in other religions that also offer salvation to all humankind, and affirming the idea that the Catholic Church is not the only means of salvation.

43. Did the Council affirm the goodness of other religions?

The Council did so, but not without a fight from its reactionary wing, which was always a small minority (10 percent or less). A number of the Council Fathers maintained that a discussion of Catholic-Jewish relations was outside the scope of the *schema* on ecumenism. Some did not want the Council to say anything on the topic. But in October, 1965, 2,080 Fathers voted on the proposition that the Jews were not cursed by God. The vote was 1,821 in the affirmative, 245 negative, and 14 invalid ballots. And with regard to the proposition regarding universal brotherhood and the exclusion of all discrimination, the vote was even stronger with 2,064 affirmative, 58 negative, and 6 invalid. Ultimately, in *Nostra Aetate,* the Declaration on the Relationship of the Church to Non-Christian Religions, the Council affirmed that "...all peoples comprise a single community and have a single origin" (No. 1) and "the Catholic Church rejects nothing which is true and holy in these [other] religions" (No. 2). As commentator Robert Graham, S.J., points out: "It is the first time an Ecumenical Council has expressed such an open approach to the other great faiths of the world."

44. Did Vatican II really resolve the Catholic Church's view of other religions once and for all?

In the church, I wonder whether anything is resolved "once and for all"? The fight over other religions still rages. On September 5, 2000, Cardinal Ratzinger, who eventually followed Cardinal Ottaviani as the head of the Holy Office, issued a white paper called *Dominus Iesus* that said the Catholic Church was the only portal to salvation, that all other religions (even the Orthodox) were defective, and that Catholics had a duty to convert them all.

Ratzinger's views were lamented. He'd turned back the clock on more than three decades of ecumenical work among all the Christian churches, and he put a damper on an ongoing dialogue with Jews, Muslims, Hindus, and Buddhists. The puzzling thing was that the pope endorsed the words of *Dominus Iesus* and then turned right around to continue his own outreach, not only to other Christians, but to Jews, Muslims, Hindus, and Buddhists.

Sadly, many of the reforms voted on at Vatican II in this area never took root. Those with traditional views are still jousting with those who want to make the church more inclusive, and they continue to criticize those who prefer to engage religions in dialogue rather than debate them. But this is just part of a fascinating story, one that began with the Incarnation itself, when the Second Person of the Trinity became man, to bring the reign of God to this earth. "The reign of God" was an expression that Jesus used many times, but it wasn't until Vatican II that theologians began plumbing the depths of meaning and the implications of Jesus' words to the vast majority of Christians. "The reign of God" finally found adequate expression in the Council's *schema* 17.

45. What did the Council mean by "the reign of God"?

The reign of God was an important biblical concept that was made new at Vatican II. In the four gospels we find Jesus used the term many times, sometimes in reference to the next world, but often to our life on earth. What did he mean when he taught us to pray "Thy Kingdom come, thy will be done on earth"? The Fathers of Vatican II answered that question by telling us that "earthly progress...is of vital concern to the Reign of God." For centuries the church had said that the Roman Catholic Church was "the Kingdom of God on earth." But that narrow notion would undergo some correction at Vatican II because the Fathers of the Council began to see that the church was not a static institution, resistant to any change or development, but an entity that was unfolding in history, compelling it to think more deeply about itself and its mission as it became more and more aware of the world around it. They suggested that we could no longer identify the church as "the Kingdom of God on earth." The church was moving toward the fullness of time and the fullness of truth, but would not reach that fullness until the Second Coming of Christ.

Theologians have a three-dollar word to describe this understanding: they call it the church's eschatological dimension (from the Greek word *eschaton,* referring to the end time). And they suggested that we had to keep this dimension in mind when we talked about the church's mission on earth. They reminded us where we were headed; at the same time, they had to insist that we hadn't arrived there yet. We still had a good deal of work ahead of us, to complete creation, to make "the Kingdom come on earth"—which means building a society devoted above all to justice and peace. And that was a task that would concern and involve the whole human race—not only Catholics, not only Christians, but also Jews and Muslims, Hindus and Buddhists. This is especially significant, given the fact that religion was the reason so many wars have been fought in the course of human history.

46. And what did the Council have to say about war and peace?

The Fathers were aware that they were breaking new ground, making "an evaluation of war with an entirely new attitude." Indeed, they reserved their most solemn language for their condemnation of modern war. "Any act of war aimed indiscriminately at the destruction of entire cities...along with their population is a crime against God and man himself. It merits unequivocal and unhesitating condemnation" (*Gaudium et Spes,* No. 80). The Council Fathers go on to state that "the unique hazard of modern warfare provides an inexorable chain of events and it can urge men into the most atrocious decisions." They begged government officials and military leaders "to give unremitting thought in their gigantic responsibility before God and the entire human race."

47. Given the Council Fathers' concerns for the issues that affect the everyday world of Catholics, did they have any discussions about contraception?

The Council Fathers did not condemn contraception in the same solemn language. In fact, they voted down the requests of some Council Fathers to do so. And Paul VI took contraception off the table, reminding the Fathers that he had delegated that issue to a special birth control commission, one that had actually been set up by John XXIII in 1963 (with only seven members), but rechartered by himself and expanded to some seventy-three experts, including married couples, demographers, sociologists, and psychologists, as well as moral theologians. But that didn't stop the Fathers from entering into a lively discussion on the ends of marriage during their discussion of *schema* 17. (It was now called *schema* 13, under a reordering and consolidation of the projects still on the table.)

48. What did Vatican II say about "the ends of marriage"?

Up until Vatican II, the official teaching of the Catholic church maintained that there was a hierarchy of the purposes for sexual intimacy in marriage—that the procreative end must be met first (that intimacy must first and foremost be open to the transmission of human life) and only then could the unitive end be met (the union between a wife and a husband). This, of course, explains the basic teaching of the church on artificial contraception—it interferes with the primary end of sexual intimacy in a marriage. However, in an effort to avoid making a judgment of the primacy of ends in marriage, *Gaudium et Spes* stated: "Hence, while not making the other purposes of matrimony of less account, the true practice of conjugal love...has this aim—that the couple be ready with stout hearts to cooperate with the love of the Creator...who through them will enlarge and enrich His own family day by day" (No. 50).

49. Did this insight from *Gaudium et Spes* pave the way for the discussions that would be held by the post-Vatican II commission on birth control?

Most definitely. The reported remarks of Cardinals Leger, Suenens, and Doepfner, now carried in full by the world press and supported by cheers for them in the conciliar hall, had a decided, if unofficial, effect on everyone, not only on those who would be appointed to the birth control commission after the Council, but on Catholics everywhere, including parish priests the world over. But this enthusiasm would be short-lived. In 1968, members of the papal birth control commission surprised Pope Paul VI by recommending a change in the church's ban on contraception. The commission said that couples had to make their own conscientious decisions on the number of their children, and that their motives were more important than their methods. One of the leading moral theologians in the commission, Jesuit Father Josef Fuchs, said that, once couples made a reasoned decision not to have any more children, they had a duty to use the most efficacious means. And a majority of the members of the birth control commission went along with Father Fuchs. They didn't prefer the rhythm method over the Pill, or the Pill over condoms or diaphragms.

50. But didn't Pope Paul VI turn his back on his own commission and reaffirm the church's traditional ban on birth control a few years later?

Yes, he did, and that decision was reaffirmed and repeated a number of times by Pope John Paul II, who had been a member of Paul VI's birth control commission, but attended none of its meetings. John Paul II spoke early and often in his reaffirmation of the solemn teaching first promulgated by Pius XI in 1931, and even made a man's position on birth control a litmus test for his appointment to the episcopacy. Even so, the vast majority of Catholic couples have made a conscientious decision in this regard and dissented from the pope's position. Some conservative commentators charge that these couples are simply disobedient. Others disagree. They say this provides us with a good example of a papal teaching that has not been "received" by the people of God. In which case, some commentators say, this is not a "teaching" at all, since few are persuaded by it. As a result, the church at large has a position at variance with the official position taken by the pope and those that follow him.

51. How can Catholics disagree with a law laid down by the pope?

There is a principle in the Catholic Church that many Catholics are not aware of. It is referred to as legitimate dissent. Basically it is a rejection of a teaching issued at the noninfallible level of official teaching. It is a very serious issue, however, and not something to be acted upon lightly. It does not advocate a kind of "cafeteria Catholicism," where one picks and chooses the teachings that one finds acceptable. It calls for serious reflection on the part of the dissenter and a competence to fully understand the teaching in question. Clearly there are those who would view every occurrence of dissent as disloyal to the church, as a form of disobedience, but that is not the case. Yes, there would be those who would abuse this principle, rationalizing a poor choice. However, this principle is for the sincere Catholic who is attempting to grow up in the faith, someone who sees that moral discernment is a matter of mature faith. In fact, legitimate dissent is rooted in the belief that the coming to truth in the church is a process that includes all the members. Responsible dissent can play a critical role in the purification and development of the church's grasp of the good news of Jesus Christ. Aware of the possibility of responsible dissent by those who are competent to evaluate this level of church teaching in a critical manner, the American bishops have offered three criteria for such dissent. They are: (1) The reasons for dissent must be serious and well-founded; (2) the manner in which one dissents must not impugn the teaching authority of the church; (3) the dissent must be such as not to give scandal.

In fact, some of the things said in the third session debate have helped guide Catholics in their dissent from official church views. Many of the Council Fathers expressed their dissent from old traditional views on the ends of marriage, and so it was no surprise to discover that Catholic lay people who read about dissent in the world press would also make their dissent known. Some Council Fathers actually objected to the church's official teaching on birth control. Perhaps no one spoke more forcefully than the Melkite Patriarch Maximos IV Saigh, who said he was only saying what married couples already knew in their hearts: that when it came to matters dealing with marital intimacy, many celibates really didn't know what they were talking about. The result: many priests around the world did stop talking about birth control. Instead, they started to encourage Catholic couples to grow up and make their own conscientious decisions over the number of children they should have. Priests who couldn't do that ended up in terrible shape, psychologically speaking. Some quit the priesthood. Even one bishop did so. Bishop James P. Shannon, auxiliary bishop of Minneapolis, left the priesthood because he could no longer hand on the church's "official teaching"—that "each and every marriage act must be open to the transmission of life." In his letter of resignation to the pope (with a copy to his own archbishop), Shannon said he had been ashamed of the advice he had been giving good Catholics, "ashamed because it has been bad theology, bad psychology, and because it has not been an honest reflection of my own inner conviction."

52. You said *schema* 13 dealt with a good many other issues concerning justice and peace?

Prior to Vatican II, there was a separation between faith and daily life. This separation can be dated back to the Protestant Reformation and the subsequent threats the church saw in such movements as the Enlightenment, with its enthronement of human reason, and the Modernist Movement, which sought to have the church engage itself with the modern world. Each of these perceived threats moved the church into a state of siege mentality, a fortress mentality in which theology was done within the "walls" of the church. But what this did was to separate the church from the world in which it lived. John XXIII, a historian in his own right, knew only too well how damaging this separation could be. The church cannot serve the people of God if it fails to take seriously the conditions of their world. *Schema* 13, which would ultimately be named *Gaudium et Spes,* the Pastoral Constitution on the Church in the Modern World, did just that. We see this in the very first line of the document: "The joys and the hopes, the griefs and the anxieties of the men (and women) of this age, especially those who are poor or in any way afflicted, these too are the joys and hopes, the griefs and anxieties of the followers of Christ. Indeed, nothing genuinely human fails to raise an echo in their hearts" (No. 1). Article three continues this point: "...this Council can provide no more eloquent proof of its solidarity with the entire human family with which it is bound up,...than by engaging with it in conversation about these various problems." This was truly a departure from previous approaches taken by the church. The whole second part of *Gaudium et Spes* dealt with what the Council Fathers considered "problems of special urgency": marriage and family, culture, economic and social life, the political community, and peace and the nations. And it would be this new approach that would pave the way for a new Christian presence in the world, a presence that would take seriously the question raised by Cain in the Book of Genesis—"Am I my brother's keeper?" Vatican II gave a definitive "yes" to Cain's question.

53. What justified the church's new involvement in justice and peace?

The church had finally come to see the world as its partner in salvation. Before Vatican II, the prevalent view of the world was a negative one. The world was somehow tainted and the church's task was to try to save that world. But a new theology of the world was emerging, one that harkened back to the first creation story of Genesis which told us that everything God created is good. It is humankind, with its ability to make choices, that distorts the goodness of the world. "Earthly progress must be carefully distinguished from the growth of Christ's kingdom. Nevertheless, to the extent that the former can contribute to the better ordering of human society, it is of vital concern to the kingdom of God" (*Gaudium et Spes,* No. 39). *Gaudium et Spes* goes on to refer to the church as "a leaven and a kind of soul for human society" (No. 40) and states that "the Catholic Church gladly holds in high esteem the things which other Christian churches or ecclesial communities have done or are doing…to achieve the same goal" (No. 40).

54. You mean the Council Fathers were pulling back on the church's traditional missionary activity?

No, but we now have a different kind of mission activity. Vatican II gave us a new understanding of the church and its mission. There was a time when we thought the Roman Catholic Church had a clear calling—to convert others to the truth, and to bring them to salvation. We had the truth, we had salvation. Others did not. Vatican II changed this way of thinking. For one thing, the Council Fathers opened the door to the value of ecumenical dialogue: discussions among differing Christian churches as well as non-Christian religions. The underlying assumption was that if God is the creator of the universe and of all humans, then the presence of God can be found everywhere on earth and in all peoples—reason enough to presume that there is a value in interfaith dialogues. This insight would have a serious impact on the way we understood the church's outreach. No longer would the primary focus of missionary activity be to simply convert others—not if we truly believed that God was already present in the world and in humanity. Our task now would be to give witness to the world of the universality of Christian redemption, to be a special Christian presence in the world.

55. What do you mean by "a special Christian presence in the world"?

Given the Council's understanding that Catholics should engage in dialogue and collaboration with followers of other religions, as well as Vatican II's position that adherents of other religions may be saved, it is clear that our former approach to missionary activity would need to be rethought. Now that activity must aim at more than the conversion of others to Roman Catholicism. Rather, the first task must be to serve as a presence of Christ among all nations, to be a sign of the universality of Christian redemption. In one of its most remarkable statements, *Gaudium et Spes* speaks of this universality. After a discussion of the gifts we receive as a result of the paschal mystery, first among them salvation, the document goes on to say: "All this holds true not only for Christians, but for all men [and women] of good will in whose hearts grace works in an unseen way. For, since Christ died for all...we ought to believe that the Holy Spirit in a manner known only to God offers to every man (and woman) the possibility of being associated with this paschal mystery" (No. 22). We must do what the word of God did—make God present to the world.

56. What did Pope Paul VI have to say about all this new thinking about the church's mission in the world?

He felt that the discussions on *schema* 13 launched the church into modern times, and this pleased him. "I am much more liberal than John XXIII," he said at the time. When the Fathers were almost finished with their discussions on *schema* 13, he came to the Council floor, simply to show his pleasure with the way things had gone. Then the Council turned to a *schema* on religious life; among all other reforms intended to bring the church up to date, religious orders, particular religious orders of women, were overdue for a change. The world was "coming of age." But nuns were still being treated like children. The conciliar draft was deemed acceptable enough for discussion, but some

Fathers criticized it when they discovered no women had been involved in writing it.

57. Why was it important for nuns to be involved in writing their own prescriptions for reform?

Because there were then twice as many nuns in the world as there were priests and some felt they ought to have a say in their future. Given all that has occurred due to the women's movement over the last twenty years, some may find it odd that this question would even be raised. Still, women in general had not yet found their voices, so it is not too surprising that women in religious orders were just beginning to develop their own identity. After all, when all of the inquiries were sent out during the preparatory phase of the Council, women were excluded from this process. It would only be at the second session of the Council, when Cardinal Suenens remarked how odd it was to be discussing matters that would affect the whole church when half of its members had no part in the deliberations, that some women would be invited to the Council as auditors. They would have no formal role, but informally they would contribute to the many theological discussions that would occur "outside" the Council proceedings among the bishops and the *periti.*

58. Is that why nuns started changing their habits?

Yes, along with many other things! And, for most, it was a welcome development. Vatican II's document on Religious Life, *Perfectae Caritatis,* called men and women in religious orders to renewal, but this renewal entailed more than a change of their religious garb. The document stated two norms to be followed: first, the following of Christ according to the gospel and second, the renewal should reflect the particular spirit and charism of the founder of the order. Before this call for renewal, members of religious orders understood themselves very differently. Obedience, humility, and docility were central virtues in the training of religious. Not that these qualities were not good; it is just that they were carried to the extreme in many cases. In addition, distortions crept into our understanding of these virtues. Obedience deteriorated in some cases into a "blind" obedience and it was held that the voice of God could always be heard in the voice of the superior. It resulted in some strange practices, like instructing a young religious to "water a stick," just to test his or her obedience. Such an activity does test something, but it is not necessarily one's obedience. Humility is another virtue that was frequently misunderstood. The film *The Nun's Story* is an example. A young woman enters the convent in Belgium prior to World War II and has great difficulty adjusting. In one scene, she is told by a superior that she should deliberately do poorly on an exam to show her humility, and to avoid the evil of human pride. The virtue of docility also succumbed to misconceptions. Rather than produce women who were open to the teachings presented to them and willing to learn, more often than not we found women who could no longer think for themselves, who were frightened of authority, and saw anything coming from an authority figure as ultimate truth. Men and women in religious orders needed to grow into a more mature living out of their vows. The Council and the renewal movement that followed would assist them greatly in this task.

59. Did the third session end on a high note?

No. As the Fathers were putting the finishing touches on *De Ecclesia,* the minority came in with some amendments that reversed the trend toward papal collaboration with the bishops in the governance of the church. And the leaders of the majority were stunned when a note was attached to *De Ecclesia* that almost made collegiality disappear. It was written at the request of the pope. Some commentators attribute his decision to a fear that the Council may have been moving too quickly and that the pope felt the need to assuage the more conservative contingent at the Council. In any event, the Fathers of the majority had no desire to fight the Holy

Father on this issue. They had won all the battles they were going to win during this third session. They were exhausted. They wanted to go home. And so there were no more objections to *De Ecclesia;* a vote on the whole document only drew nineteen dissenting votes. *De Ecclesia* came down to compromising or having no document at all. The majority resigned themselves to reality.

Then their resignation turned into gloom when the Council moderators pulled back, again, from the Declaration on Religious Liberty. The document that was now before the Council was so different from what had gone before that it called for a new debate. The pope agreed. The majority had two more setbacks: they found that other, eleventh-hour changes had been made to both of Cardinal Bea's prime projects: the Decree on Ecumenism and the Declaration on Non-Christian Religions (which now contained the old *schema* on the Jews). There were more compromises, probably granted to the minority by the vacillating pope, but the Fathers felt they had no choice. They voted almost unanimously to pass the Decree on Ecumenism, and put off until the fourth session the Declaration on Non-Christian Religions. The Council had wasted so much time on matters of far less importance. Now they knew full well they had to come back to Rome again for a fourth session.

Six

Fourth Session: September 14–December 8, 1965

Compromise and Reform, A Mixed Conclusion

60. Did the Council Fathers feel better when they finally saw the end in sight?

Decidedly. In the fourth session, the Council Fathers put the final touches on the *schemata* dealing with reform of the religious life and priestly formation in the seminaries. But some of the majority were miffed when the pope banned any discussion of priestly celibacy, and said he would insist on the observance of celibacy in the Western Church. Many priests had actually believed that, since celibacy was a mere discipline in the church (that is, man-made), men could and would change it (in the spirit of all the other freedoms being promulgated by and with and through the Council). When it became clear right after the Council that there would be no change, priests began leaving the priesthood in the thousands. A good many nuns did so as well. In the years since the Council, the church has seen a serious decline in vocations to the priesthood and religious life and many today believe this is the central crisis facing the church of the new millennium.

61. What documents were finally approved and promulgated at the fourth session?

Most of the Council Fathers were smiling as the fourth and final session ended. It had opened on September 14, 1965, and by the time it ended on December 8, 1965, it proved to be the most active of the sessions. It issued two constitutions: *Dei Verbum,* the Dogmatic Constitution on Divine Revelation, and *Gaudium et Spes,* the Dogmatic Constitution on the Church in the Modern World; six decrees: *Christus Dominus,* Decree Concerning the Pastoral Office of Bishops in the Church; *Perfectae Caritatis,* Decree on Renewal of Religious Life; *Optatum Totius,* Decree on Priestly Training; *Apostolicam Actuositatem,* Decree on the Apostolate of the Laity; *Ad Gentes,* Decree on the Missionary Activity of the Church; and *Presbyterorum Ordinis,* Decree on the Ministry and Life of Priests; and three declarations: *Gravissimum Educationis,* Declaration on Christian Education; *Nostra Aetate,* Declaration on the Relation of the Church to Non-Christian Religions; and *Dignitatis Humanae,* Declaration on Religious Freedom.

The second and third sessions of the Council, both held under Pope Paul VI, had ended under a cloud and it was assumed that the fourth session would probably end in like fashion. Yet, as Council commentator Francis X. Murphy points out, Vatican II came to a close on December 7 and 8 on an extremely positive note, the chief credit for this going to Pope Paul VI, who was carefully planning the strategy of the closing days.

62. Why was it important for the Fathers to pass a statement on the Jews?

Nostra Aetate, the Declaration on the Relationship of the Church to Non-Christian Religions, was an unexpected outcome of the Council. In the early stages, the only reference to non-Christian religions was found in the first draft of the Decree on Ecumenism. What occurred in the sessions preceding the drafting and promulgation of *Nostra Aetate* was a process in which the Council Fathers unlearned a number of prejudices and slowly came to realize a number of truths.

Perhaps the most significant aspect of this document's treatment of the Jews was the sustained attempt to determine the place of the Jewish people in the plan of salvation history. Important, as well, was the fact that it rejected the notion that the Jewish people as a whole ever did bear responsibility for the crucifixion and it deplored any expression of anti-Semitism.

That "the Jewish question" was even given a place on the Council's agenda is remarkable. Some Councils in the past had discussed Jews and Judaism, but primarily in a negative light. Never before had a systematic and positive presentation of Jews and Judaism been made in the church by a pope or a council. Commentators credit this achievement to Pope John XXIII who made the decision to include it on the agenda for Vatican II and, perhaps more important, for managing to keep it there.

63. What was the significance of *Dignitatis Humanae,* Vatican II's Declaration on Religious Freedom?

The final text of this document emerged only after much deliberation, frequently quite contentious. Its significance in the life of the church cannot be overestimated, especially when one considers the history of the church in this regard. Before Vatican II, Catholics were restricted in their freedom of belief, public testimony, worship, and moral discernment by authoritative forces in the church. Virtually all policy-making decisions were held by clerics. Theological inquiry and expression were also subject to control. By any number of means, the community of belief had its freedom curtailed. The Declaration on Religious Freedom represents a major advance in church thinking on this issue. The Council Fathers insisted on the inviolable right of every human person, because of his or her inherent dignity, to profess and practice a religious faith without coercion. The truth was to be offered, not enforced.

64. How did the Council end?

After all the voting was over, and all the amendments made, and all *schemata* had been given their final re-rewrites, Paul VI was anxious to demonstrate that the Roman Curia had not subdued his own reforming spirit. He announced that he would institute a synod of bishops that would meet on a regular basis. He hoped that regular synods would enhance the participation of the bishops in setting policies for the church (though no one used the word "democracy"). The pope also announced a reform of the Holy Office, which he signaled by changing its name to the Congregation for the Doctrine of the Faith. But these synods have turned out to be major disappointments because the bishops were only given a mandate to advise the pope, not to have an active participation in his decisions, and because Pope John Paul II takes a very active role in the synods. Some bishops have said that they felt intimidated by his presence at each synod, a move that made them hesitant to speak their minds. Others said they would have appreciated a synodal presence by some of the church's great theologians, but, as a matter of policy, John Paul's synods had no *periti* in Rome.

Pope Paul VI presided over the final public session on December 7. He took the occasion to remove the excommunication levied in 1054 against the patriarch of Constantinople. And, that night, the pope thanked the *periti* for their yeoman service. He also urged them to go on talking to their bishops, as they had learned to do so well in Rome during Vatican II.

SEVEN

THE CHURCH RIGHT AFTER THE COUNCIL—THE EARLY YEARS

65. What happened after the Council?

The first thing everyone noticed was that the Mass had changed, almost overnight. The Council Fathers wanted to make the liturgy more simple, more participatory, more intelligible, and more dynamic. For centuries, priests had taken their places at a high altar with their backs to the people while they murmured the words of the Mass like an incantation, and in Latin besides. Now priests all over the world left their high altars and set up simple tables closer to the people—and they faced the people. Instead of whispering the prayers in Latin, they read them aloud in the language (and even the dialects) of the people, from a soft Austrian German to a clicking African Zulu. The words struck the listeners as more conversational, so that the Mass became less like a ritual and more like a banquet. Primitive worship had been essentially communal, and now Catholics were encouraged to think communally once more. They were told this was their Mass, too, and Masses got noisier. They were urged to pocket their rosaries, join in the prayers of the priest, and to greet their neighbors with a kiss of peace. They started receiving communion wafers in the hand. Some laymen became deacons and preached homilies. Laymen and laywomen were recruited as lectors and they helped distribute communion, too. Mass became more of a happy celebration than a solemn ceremony, and priests replaced their old, lugubrious, black Requiem Mass for the Dead with Masses of the Resurrection for their loved ones who had, after all, just gone home to God.

Of course, not everyone was at home with all the changes and the Council Fathers made things even worse for those uncomfortable with change by making provisions for further changes and adaptation. They allowed for legitimate adaptations to different groups, regions, and peoples. And they left it to the bishops of each region to determine which elements from the traditions of their people might appropriately be admitted into divine worship.

Few bishops actually did that. Ever since the Council of Trent, the liturgy had undergone little or no change. And in the canon of the Mass, which begins right after the "Holy, holy, holy," there had been no change at all until Pope John XXIII added the name of St. Joseph to the prayer at the beginning of this part of the Mass. Few remembered that during the church's first fifteen centuries the liturgy was subject to a constant process of change provoked by cultural and social forces. All they had were the prescriptions of the Council of Trent, which set down rigid rubrics that no one could alter. After Vatican II, most bishops (who had had their training in seminaries fashioned by a good number of Tridentine rigidities) seemed incapable of making liturgical adaptations.

66. How were the changes put forth at the Council explained to the faithful?

Sadly, not very well at all. Much depended upon one's local parish. In some cases, the local clergy had followed the Council's proceedings and were enthusiastic. This knowledge and enthusiasm were then passed on to parishioners. Unfortunately, such parishes were in the minority. Most Catholics right after the Council simply were not educated about the reasons for the changes. As a result, reactions varied. Those who were given the theological rationale behind the changes liked them. Those who didn't sufficiently understand the reason, or worse, weren't given any reasons at all, were just confused.

67. Overall, how was Vatican II received by the hierarchy? The people in the pews?

Vatican II was clearly not an overnight success story! One of the reasons for this was stated earlier. After the teaching on papal infallibility had been articulated by Vatican I in 1869–1870, no one in the church thought we would ever see another Church Council, much less need one. So the announcement of Vatican II by John XXIII in 1959 caught most Catholics off guard, including the hierarchy. Catholic seminaries and convents were filled, as were Catholic schools. Catholic identity was extremely high. The attitude among many church leaders was concern that this Council would simply open up a "Pandora's Box." No doubt many of them mused: "What on earth has this pope got in mind?" The overall reception of the Council's teachings and suggested changes would depend in large part on a number of factors.

The history of the church indicates that most of the great councils were followed by periods of confusion. But Vatican II differed from past councils, a difference that would clearly add to the confusion one might normally expect. Previous church councils sought to restore the church's internal stability and produce a stronger dogmatic front. Vatican II did just the opposite. It looked to relax past rigidity and bring about an opening to the world. It sought to create a church less focused on itself as an institution and more focused on its people. Such goals would naturally produce a sense of instability. As noted by theologian Joseph Komonchak, the church of the previous century was known for its emphasis on uniformity and by its centralization of authority in Rome. But Vatican II called these values into question. He considers Vatican II a historic cultural turning point for Roman Catholicism in that substantial institutional and theological reforms, which had been resisted for centuries, were now being given such serious attention. Is it any wonder that the years right after the Council witnessed such confusion?

68. Confusion seems to be the dominant experience of Catholics after the Council. Was Vatican II's particular time in history a factor in this confusion?

Most definitely. The Council ended in 1965 in the middle of perhaps the most turbulent decade America had seen in the twentieth century. Those old enough can recall the 1960s as a time of the Vietnam war, of protest and unrest, a time when every expression of authority would come under scrutiny. The church would not escape this scrutiny and, into this turbulent state of affairs, the Catholic church, through its sixteen documents, offered a self-portrait that lacked the certitude of the pre-Vatican II church that acknowledged past failures of all members (including the clergy), a portrait that no longer offered the triumphalistic assurance of having the fullness of truth, but confessed humbly before its God and its members that the church truly is a pilgrim people, on the way to the fullness of truth. The combination of a society in disarray and a church admitting its limitations was sure to produce great confusion among most Catholics.

69. Didn't religious education right after the Council address this confusion?

In a word, no. In fact, it would prove to have a detrimental effect. Perhaps sociologist Father Andrew Greeley had the best take on the problem. (See Timothy G. McCarthy, *The Catholic Tradition: Before and After Vatican II 1878–1993* [Chicago: Loyola University Press, 1994], p. 76.) Though Vatican II saw itself as a pastoral council, no real attempt was made at the Council to develop new catechetical styles for teaching the gospel to the generation after Vatican II, nor did it seem to take into consideration the actual religious needs of the members at the time—especially in light of the changes that would occur. The primary tool of religious education just prior to the Council was the Baltimore Catechism, which had an authoritarian catechetical style. Such an approach was very effective before Vatican II. Know the answers to the questions and you have the faith. Of course, as stated above, the 1960s would replace this admiration for authority.

70. So why did the catechism style of teaching fail us after the Council?

One of the most important developments to take place at Vatican II was the renewed emphasis on personal conscience and the role it might play in moral discernment. There would be serious implications once Catholics would exercise the privileges of conscience, and not enough thought went into how we might prepare the members for such concerns.

For one thing, Catholics before the Council were discouraged from raising questions about the faith. It was deemed disobedient and disloyal. And, though in principle we officially held the primacy of conscience, we really did not talk about it very much. The church just before the Council has been referred to as paternalistic—treating the members the way parents treat their children. And, given the times, this was understandable. Church leaders were clearly well-intentioned. But their thinking was also colored by an Augustinian kind of thinking. After his conversion, St. Augustine came to believe that the human condition was basically "depraved" due to original sin. This led to a rather pessimistic view of the human condition—that humans somehow need to be protected from themselves, the way a parent protects a child from childhood ignorance. John XXIII, on the other hand, approached the human condition with an optimism of grace, focusing more on the power of God in the human person. We were not prepared for the complications that would emerge when Catholics took the teaching on conscience to heart. Almost overnight, new freedoms would be available. Our new appreciation for individual conscience would require a new approach in religious education. The catechism could no longer meet our needs.

71. What took the place of the catechism?

Frequently, the move away from one extreme results in a swing to the opposite extreme. Clearly this was the case in religious education after the Council. Anxious to move away from a juridical, law-oriented, black-and-white approach to the faith, the period right after Vatican II witnessed the opposite. God was no longer someone to be feared. God was Love—so loving, in fact, that some were moved to claim that eternal punishment was no longer a reality to take seriously. Balloons and smiley faces were everywhere (forgetting, I suppose, that the central symbol of Christianity is a cross, not a smiley face)! Feeling good about oneself seemed to replace the need to honestly evaluate the status of one's journey to God. And learning the content of the faith was somehow lost in the exuberance. We forgot that the mature act of faith requires both head and heart knowledge. As a result, the generations of Catholics in the years right after the Council left their religious education centers feeling good about their God, their world, and themselves, but possessing precious little of the theological underpinnings of the faith that would be needed to sustain the faith in the years to come.

72. What happened to the Blessed Mother after Vatican II?

The Fathers of the Council tried to help us get our priorities straight. Some listened to them; many Catholics moved away from an excessive devotion to Mary and the saints in the direction of a more New Testament Christianity centered on Jesus, which was quite a turnaround. Preconciliar Catholics had had a deep devotion to Mary, to May processions, and the crowning of Mary as Queen of Heaven. In some elementary schools, children would even write at the heading of all their assignments "to Jesus through Mary," assuming that the only way to reach God was through the intercession of the Mother of God. Almost everyone recited the Rosary, and some American families did it together every night, convinced by an energetic media campaign conducted by a priest of the Holy Cross named Patrick Peyton that "the family that prays together stays together." In 1943, Hollywood took an inspiring tale about the miracles of Lourdes and made it into a hit movie, *The Song of*

Bernadette. In the same era, Catholics customarily called upon St. Anthony to find lost objects and placed St. Christopher medals on the dashboards of their cars to get them home safely. Some Catholics believed that wearing a small square of brown wool next to their breast (it was called a *scapular*) at the moment of death assured them a quick pass into heaven. Many of the Fathers at Vatican II felt that devotions like these, especially to Mary and the saints, were excessive and at times superstitious. Asked during the Council's first session to endorse a pietistic declaration of devotion to Mary, they refused. (The pope didn't want to make an issue of it; he went off and promulgated a Marian statement all by himself.) Later in the Council, rather than devote an entire Council document to Mary alone, the bishops included their statement on Mary in one chapter of *Lumen Gentium,* the Dogmatic Constitution on the Church.

The bishops hoped to show that in spite of the unique role played by Mary in the plan of salvation, she is still to be seen as a member of the church, not some kind of semi-deity, as Catholics did in some countries, to the fascination and fear of tourists from Protestant lands. The Council Fathers (anxious to build bridges to other Christians, whom they now called "separated brethren") were trying to take a middle ground between two extremes. They held that Mary should continue to be venerated above all the saints because of her status as the Mother of the Redeemer, but frowned on an exaggerated devotion that made Mary into a goddess.

73. Did the Council Fathers take the same approach toward the veneration of the saints?

Along with novenas, rosaries, the Nine First Fridays and all-night devotion to the Blessed Sacrament, devotion to the saints seems to be on the wane in our time (although there are pockets of nostalgic Catholicism where the folk, even young folk, cherish these things). Our churches used to be filled with statues of the saints. We used to chant the Litany of the Saints on special occasions. We used to memorize the feast days of all the saints (and I can still recite most of them by heart). We used to wear St. Christopher medals on silver chains around our necks. I think we may have simply grown out of this phase of Catholic history.

I am afraid the Council Fathers did not have much to say about the saints. Oh, they gave them their due in Vatican II's document *Lumen Gentium.* They encouraged the faithful to seek the intercession of the saints and to ask their assistance in obtaining blessings from God, and told us that the saints serve as a reminder of God's presence in the world. But they also urged us to avoid exaggerated devotions. In this regard, the Holy House of Loreto comes to mind. Purportedly it is the home where the Angel Gabriel declared to Mary that she would be the Mother of Our Lord, which somehow moved miraculously from the Holy Land to Italy.

There are a number of reasons why the Council Fathers had their reservations about the saints. Modern church historians had exposed many of the saints as pious figures who were often the products of overactive imaginations. The Bollandists of Belgium, a group of Jesuit historians, discovered that St. Philomena and St. Christopher never existed, or rather, existed only in the realm of misty myth. Rome removed them from the official calendar of saints, to the great dismay of their devotees.

There are even a number of theologians today who question the relevance of the canonization process, but I think we still need saints. We all revel in heroes and heroines, men and women very much like us who give witness to the goodness of God and this world by the very lives they live, whether they are single, or celibate, or married. It would be so hard to be hopeful in our world without them. Perhaps Karl Rahner, one of the greatest theologians of the twentieth century, said it best: "Saints are the initiators and creative models of the holiness which happens to be right for…their particular age. They prove that a certain form of life…is a really genuine possibility" (Thomas Bokenkotter, *Dynamic Catholicism* [Doubleday: New York], p. 157).

74. The architecture of churches changed after Vatican II, didn't it?

Right after the Council, we saw the construction of new churches and chapels that corrected the architectural abuses, dating all the way back to the medieval church, where rood screens were erected between the priests celebrating Mass and the people in the pews. Only those in the choir stalls and the nobility actually saw what was happening on the altar, or had a chance to gaze on (but generally not partake of) the sacred host. New church architecture in the postconciliar era corrected that; many churches took on a circular shape, where the people experienced Mass-in-the-round, with nary a statue in anyone's line of sight.

But some took simplicity to an extreme. I know of one chapel that was built without a single statue in it, and very few images of any kind. Their stations of the cross are numbers on the wall, one to fourteen, and nothing more. This was in reaction, I suspect, to the spectacle of churches that were crammed with images lacking any real artistic sense and copies of the Infant Jesus of Prague with as many changes of wardrobe as Barbie and Ken dolls.

75. In some cases, church music also went to the same extremes as church architecture, didn't it?

Yes, unfortunately. Liturgical music after the Council fell victim to the same lack of readiness as other facets of church life. The melodic, majestic Gregorian Chant found itself challenged by a new musical genre: the folk Mass. And in place of the serious and calming sounds of the organ, Catholics found themselves jolted by guitars, trumpets, tambourines, and drums at their Sunday Mass. "What happened to my church?" was a question on the lips of many Catholics just after local parishes introduced the liturgical changes. Coupled with this "new sound" was a larger problem. Some of the first hymns heard at the folk Masses sounded more like children's songs than a form of prayer. Many missed the beauty of pre-Vatican II music, not finding the new hymns conducive for praying.

76. It seems that Vatican II was a confusing blessing for the church. Did it receive any negative reactions?

Most definitely. And the reasons for the opposition vary. There were those who maintained that the Council's teachings were not in keeping with the tradition of the church. Another voice of opposition came from those who professed obedience to the hierarchy but who still longed for a return to the kind of church experienced under Pope Pius XII. Perhaps the person best remembered for his rejection of Vatican II is Archbishop Marcel Lefebvre of France. In 1970 he established the Fraternity of Pius X, a staunchly conservative group. In a document sent to the group in 1974, Lefebvre rejected what he called the Rome of neo-Modernist and neo-Protestant leanings that showed themselves at the Council. The highpoint of his opposition occurred when he claimed that the Council had turned its back on tradition and was, therefore, a schismatic Council. In follow-up statements Lefebvre was less antagonistic, but experienced no real change in his position. He was suspended by Pope Paul VI in 1976 and excommunicated in 1988 when he ordained four bishops in his Fraternity.

In one sense, the Council documents actually contributed to the poor reception they received by some members in the church. Two tendencies were clearly at work at the Council and, to use the well-known terms, these would be the conservative and the liberal. As a result, the documents do not present a totally unified picture. One can find evidence of both tendencies in the documents. Commentators have called them interim or transitional documents. And perhaps this is why Karl Rahner referred to Vatican II as "the beginning of the beginning" (Robert Burns, O.P., *Roman Catholicism: Yesterday and Today* [Chicago: Loyola University Press, 1992], p. 41).

77. After so many years, are there still those who reject Vatican II?

Absolutely. We continue to see pockets of resistance today, people who claim that the decades following Vatican II have been chaotic, filled with developments that are detrimental to the church, and they lay the blame on the Second Vatican Council. They point to the shortage of vocations to the priesthood and religious life, the decline in Mass attendance and reception of the sacrament of penance, and the tensions between theologians and the hierarchy as evidence of the demise. And they suggest the solution lies in a return to the pre-Vatican II model of church. In a sense, their claim is understandable. The previous model of church offered stability and certitude. The current model is not so neat. Those who reject Vatican II prefer a church that is more a hierarchical institution than a communion and emphasize papal authority. They miss novenas, Forty Hours, May processions, the Latin Mass. In those days, according to writer Garry Wills, Catholicism was a "vast set of intermeshed childhood habits...chants, christenings, grace at meals; beads, altar, incense, candles....All these things were shared, part of community life...It was a ghetto, undeniably. But not a bad ghetto to grow up in" (Garry Wills, *Bare Ruined Choirs: Doubt, Prophecy, and Radical Religion* [Garden City, N.Y.: Doubleday, 1971], pp. 15, 37).

And then came the turbulent 1960s and the Second Vatican Council. The Catholicism of the 1950s would undergo many changes, not all of them good. So, I do understand the reluctance of the opposition to embrace Vatican II. However, two points should be made. First, one of the central fears of the opposition is that the church no longer espouses eternal truths. But that is not the case. The basic truths given in Revelation do not change. Rather, the human family grows in its understanding of these truths. Second, the history of the church shows us that in every era the church has experienced theological unrest. We tend to forget this and focus unduly on our own time. We can go back to the beginning, in A.D. 49, when the early church called its first Council in Jerusalem to settle the thorny problem of the admission of

Gentiles into the Christian community and how that would affect the observance of Mosaic laws. We might do well to recall one very wise statement used by John XXIII: "In essential things, unity; in doubtful things, liberty; in all things, charity."

78. What is the authority of the sixteen Vatican II documents? Are Catholics bound to obey them?

As theologian Robert Burns, O.P. has pointed out, Vatican II was different from any previous church council in that it did not specify any of its teachings as dogma in a formal sense. But he adds that no responsible Catholic theologian would publicly deny them as the teachings of the church. The documents are listed under three different categories: constitutions, declarations, and decrees. Overall, the conciliar teachings were presented as pastoral guidance for the church and are to be accepted by Roman Catholics. None are completely "new." Rather, they offer a deeper understanding of existing teachings.

79. As the years passed after the Council, do you think the church suffered any damage or loss of credibility?

I would have to say yes. There has been a general loss of trust in the church on the part of many Catholics, particularly Catholic youth. It isn't because they despise religion. Most people (and their numbers in the United States are increasing after September 11, 2001) have a deep yearning for the transcendent. They look to God for blessings, and they say they pray—every day.

Polls tell us that 90 percent of the population believe in life after death. But they lack faith in the church, or indeed, in any organized Christian religion. A large number of Catholics under the age of forty no longer regard themselves as formal members of the church. Some divorced and remarried Catholics, seeing no hope for their situation, simply drift away. Many Catholics who do persevere reject the official teaching of the church on issues that have anything to do with sex, and they simply do not understand many other articles of faith, such as the Real Presence. They are appalled by the stories of male clergy who are caught abusing children, a phenomenon some link to enforced celibacy. They are amazed over the church's failure to face up to the serious shortage of priests. Some claim that the church is simply bearing the brunt of trying to faithfully bring the Word of God to a skeptical society. But that's the society that this church has to reach. If the society doesn't believe in the kind of authority that says, "Believe it because I say so," then the church needs to commend itself by a different kind of authority, an authority that preaches not so much with words, but by example. The New York City firemen who trooped into the crumbling Twin Towers to their own destruction have authority not because of what they said, or say, but because of what they did, and do. If the church as institution isn't making an impact on society, then it must look at itself and ask why. Men and women of the church (laypeople as well as priests and religious) need not be perfect exemplars of every human virtue. But they should be and could be making more of an impact on our world. And no amount of human weakness, failure, or even sin should get in the way of the instructions of the risen Christ given in the twenty-eighth chapter of Matthew's Gospel: "Go, therefore, and make disciples of all nations, baptizing them in the name of the Father, and of the Son and of the Holy Spirit, teaching them to observe all that I have commanded you. And, lo, I am with you always, to the close of the age."

There is an important theological principle based on this scripture reference, one that could "rehabilitate" the church's credibility. It is the indefectibility principle. The quote from Matthew's Gospel is an assurance from the risen Christ that sin will never so dominate the church that it could be totally unfaithful to God's truth. In essence, the church is a mystery in that it includes both divine and human elements. Because of the human component, the church is not perfect, nor will it ever be. The words of the risen Christ assure us that, despite our sinfulness, error will not have the final word, even though partial errors and human failure are always possible. Vatican II gave clear support to this principle in *Gaudium et Spes:* "Although, by the power of the Holy Spirit the church has remained the faithful spouse of her Lord and has never ceased to be the sign of salvation on earth, she is still very aware...how great a distance lies between the message she offers and the human failings of those to whom the Gospel is entrusted" (No. 43).

80. Anyone familiar with the post-conciliar church knows that the Council triggered a radical split between conservatives and liberals. How can we see the Council as good when it has created this split?

Catholic journals and periodicals tell us a great deal about the tension that came about between two groups in the church in the years after Vatican II. They are known by many names: the right and the left, the open and the closed, progressives and those holding established positions, the classicist and the historically conscious, the pre-Vatican II thinkers and the post-Vatican II thinkers. But when it comes right down to it, we generally find ourselves using terminology that actually fosters the tension: liberal versus conservative. Neither of these terms is very useful. Both are stereotypes and stereotypes are rarely fair. The fact is that theologians (and a good many laypeople) are split on some issues, and both sides use the documents to support their positions. This not only makes for a contentious climate in the church; it also causes a great deal of confusion for the average Catholic, especially those old enough to remember a solidly unified picture before the Council.

Before Vatican II, most Catholics knew what it meant to be Catholic, and what their church taught. One commentator said of this period: "Prick one Catholic and we all bleed." Uniformity was assured by conformity. But that uniformity has broken down and many claim that Catholicism enters the twenty-first century in a divided state. How did this happen? Is it destructive to the faith? Is there a solution?

To understand this issue, we have to go back to John XXIII's initial calling of the Council, the reaction of many to this announcement, and the theological mindset of the representatives gathered for the Council sessions. Inside the Vatican, administrators of the curial offices expressed amazement and surprise that the pope would even call a Council. "The pope's infallible," they said. "He can solve any problem with a stroke of his pen." Men who thought like this must have been living at a level of abstraction that wasn't human. How could the pastoral-minded bishops who came to the Council from all over the world even relate to them?

These pastors tried to understand the administrators, of course, and learned to sympathize with them when they realized that those administrators were paralyzed with fear that the reforms afoot would change their lives forever, and possibly even make them and their jobs unnecessary. Quite often, it was the administrators who were comfortable with the pyramidal model of the church, where truth and authority were centered in their offices in Rome. To them, the word *church* was frequently identified with the hierarchy, or, as they liked to call it, *la chiesa stessa,* the church itself—as if they were the church and everyone else just belonged to it.

Most of the pastorally-minded bishops at Vatican II, many of them missionaries, followed a second model, one that was more open to change. Revolutionary? Not really. Their model dated all the way back to the primitive church already described in the letters of the Apostle Paul. They favored a definition of church as the family of the "people of God." And they used another word, *communio,* to describe the kind of open communication that ought to go on with the church family. These pastors tended to listen more to laypeople because they felt that in this *communio* all the members of the church, by virtue of their baptism, could be sources of truth since the Holy Spirit was given to each of us, whether priests, religious, or lay.

81. Given the certitude that the pre-Vatican II church offered, isn't it natural that certain tensions would emerge?

Of course. When we say "We believe," we are placing our hope and trust in that which is yet unseen and unproven. Unfortunately, catechism Catholicism lulled us into a false sense of security, and taught us to accept certain answers before we even had questions. Worse, the catechism kept us in a kind of infantile state, and prevented us from asking any of the hard questions that must necessarily precede a genuine faith commitment as part of our covenant with God. Our teachers did not encourage us to ask questions as a necessary step in our authentic search for God; instead, they told us that our questions demonstrated that we were wanting in obedience and docility, two central qualities of the pre-Vatican II Catholic. After a while, even the most earnest of believers chose silence as the lesser evil.

I believe Vatican II helped change that. The Fathers at Vatican II did not "create" a new theology. They rediscovered a theology rooted in the New Testament and went about discarding some of the distorted notions that had crept into Christianity over the years. Old catechisms maintained that the Catholic Church was the only portal to salvation. The Fathers at Vatican II bowed down humbly before the gracious mystery we call God and placed concerns that our finite human natures cannot fully comprehend into the hands of God. They took seriously the words of Jesus in the seventh chapter of Matthew's Gospel: "If you then who are wicked know how to give good things to your children, how much more will your heavenly Father give good things to those who ask him?" This unconditional love of the Father is clearly understood in Article 22 of *Gaudium et Spes*. After some paragraphs on the paschal mystery and what Christians receive as a result of this mystery, the document states: "All this holds true not only for Christians, but for all men of good will in whose hearts grace works in an unseen way. For, since Christ died for all men...we ought to believe that the Holy Spirit in a manner known only to God offers to every man the possibility of being associated with this Paschal Mystery."

82. Did Vatican II also change the catechism's previous thinking about vocations?

Yes. Rather than place the holiness of the celibate lifestyle above all others, *Lumen Gentium,* the Dogmatic Constitution on the Church, stated: "Thus it is evident to everyone that all the faithful of Christ of whatever rank or status are called to the fullness of Christian life and to the perfection of charity" (No. 40). Yet, some may remember a catechism page alluded to elsewhere in this text that shows two pictures: one, a couple getting married with the claim above it, "This is good." Right next to this is a photo of a nun praying. The caption read: "This is better."

The Baltimore Catechism was published in 1885 and it represented the sixteenth-century theology of the Council of Trent, an understanding of the faith that had centuries to solidify and take root in the heads of believers. But Vatican II discovered insights into the faith that would enable us to rethink and rearticulate our understanding of Catholicism. So it should come as no surprise that many Catholics were at first rather reluctant to embrace the cautious, humble, tentative approach to the faith emerging from the Council, an approach based on the recognition that God is best defined as mystery. The pre-Vatican II mindset that we already had all the answers was verging on arrogance.

83. It seems that some important shifts in the church's self-understanding occurred at Vatican II, changes that would require Catholics to rethink the faith as well. Do you agree?

Yes. Vatican II has been called a "self-study" by the church. By being so named, it gains in credibility because it is seen as more selfless, and more at the service of the people. This is part of the renewal and reform that Blessed Pope John XXIII tried to promote at Vatican II. When he did that, he set in motion a good deal of new theologizing that would affect our whole notion of faith. The Council helped to recall the distinction between the content of the faith and the human act of faith, which must entail a personal self-surrender to the God revealed in the person of Jesus Christ, whom we view as the human face of God. Faith is not simply an intellectual assent to a body of truths given to us in Revelation. Simply saying yes to the taught dogmas and doctrines of our religion will not qualify us as faithful, faith-filled Catholics. Something more is needed. Genuine faith requires that my intellectual knowledge about God will affect my life. This personal act of faith can only occur when God becomes a reality; when I consciously enter into a relationship with my God. And this is not a once-and-for-all moment. Fidelity—whether toward God or another person—requires the journey of a lifetime. It really is a falling in love with God who first loved us. And it calls for an awareness of and acceptance of the God who is truly present in the core of my being. Like a woman who discovers she is with child, we discover the presence of the God who has been within us all along, waiting for us to say yes. Our pre-Vatican II approach, which could be called "an affair of the intellect," gave way after the Council to "an affair of the heart." But we need both!

Vatican II did not totally discard the pre-Vatican II understanding of faith, because the best articulation regarding faith in our tradition has always recognized the need for a personal acceptance of Revelation. However, over the years we neglected the personal dimension. And one new emphasis can be discerned in the Council's teaching. It stressed the freedom of faith—on God's side and ours. Article 2 of *Dignitatis Humanae,* the Declaration on Religious Freedom, states: "This freedom means that all men are to be immune from coercion…in such wise that in matters religious no one is to be forced to act in a manner contrary to his own beliefs...that the right to religious freedom has its foundation in the very dignity of the human person." This is a far cry from the time when we held that Christianity should be the religion of the state and actually engaged in coercive activity to bring this about.

Article 1 of the Declaration also claims that "the truth cannot impose itself except by virtue of its own truth." Curious. The church fought the Enlightenment for 200 years. And then, at Vatican II, it seemed to adopt and adapt a key idea of Denis Diderot, an Enlightenment thinker: "The mind can only acquiesce in what it accepts as true. The heart can only love what seems good to it. Violence will turn a man into a hypocrite if he is weak and into a martyr if he is strong. Teaching, persuasion and prayer, these are the only legitimate means of spreading the faith" (J. Livingston, *Modern Christian Thought* [New York: Macmillan, 1971], p. 8).

EIGHT

THE CHURCH TODAY—THE LEGACY OF VATICAN II

84. Given what you have said about the early years right after the Council, it seems as though theology changed almost overnight. Was that the case?

Hardly. Remarkable theologians like Congar and Chenu, de Lubac and Danielou, Schillebeeckx and Rahner had been doing their research and reflection for decades before the Council. They were men of great theological vision and insight, but their work was deemed dangerous by those inside the Vatican who were guarding the deposit of the faith so their work was suppressed—until Vatican II, when its chief architects turned to them for the key ideas that would help them bring the church up-to-date, and trigger three major shifts in theology that continue to have a significant impact on the way we do theology today. These shifts, which have a direct bearing on the way we live as Christians today, deal with our worldview, our theological method, and the way we convey the gospel to others.

85. Theology has a new worldview?

Theologians speak about a shift from a classicist worldview to a historically conscious worldview. The traditional classicist view maintained the truth of the past as certain and unchangeable for every future time and culture. Vatican II substituted the historically-conscious view which holds that every expression of a theological truth is historically conditioned. John XXIII, who was trained more as an historian than a theologian, said that truths themselves are not affected by history. But he implied that each new age presents new data, new questions, new discoveries that theologians must think about when they seek to give reasons for our hope. Ongoing revelation is a term used to describe this approach.

86. I am confused. You said that the truths of Revelation do not change. How then can Revelation be "ongoing"?

Perhaps one of the most misunderstood aspects of Catholic faith deals with the way God has been revealed to our world. Exactly what is Revelation? Where do we find it, and how does it reach humanity? How do we pass it on in each generation? We have to elaborate answers to these basic questions if the reality of Revelation is to have any meaning in our lives.

Basically, the word *Revelation* refers to what God has revealed about himself to creation. In fact, we all engage in this kind of activity as well when we reveal something about ourselves to others. *Dei Verbum,* Vatican II's Dogmatic Constitution on Divine Revelation, made a remarkable contribution to the way we speak about Revelation today. Revelation is often referred to as the "truths of the faith" and as the "ancient deposit of faith." The way we dealt with these truths underwent a profound theological development at the Council. Prior to Vatican II, we viewed this "deposit of faith" in a static, unchanging manner. We believed that these truths were given to us once and for all by God and were to be passed on to each new generation in the very same way we received them. The way they were first understood and articulated in the earliest of times enjoyed a kind of permanent, eternal status. But Vatican II provided us with an exciting insight in this regard. Ongoing revelation is the term used to describe this insight. The term has caused a bit of controversy among some theologians but I believe that is due to a misunderstanding. What does it claim about the truths that God has revealed? Basically this: the Christian God is best described as mystery, a richness of meaning so deep that the finite human can never fully comprehend this fullness who is God. As a result, human language about God always falls short. Natural language simply breaks down when discussing the supernatural. Hence, no doctrine, no creedal statement, no council document can ever capture this mystery in its entirety. Ongoing revelation claims that God initiated the conversation with humanity and revealed certain truths. And Christianity holds that Scripture and Tradition are the two formal sources of these truths.

Ongoing revelation has disturbed some theologians because to them it sounds as though the truths themselves undergo change, thereby bringing about a kind of relativism, so that somehow there are no absolute truths given by God. But that is not the claim of ongoing revelation. "Ongoing" refers not to the truths themselves but to the way humans come to grasp these truths. In other words, we grow in our understanding of what God has revealed. Over the course of time, humanity comes to a deeper and deeper understanding of the "deposit of faith." It is the way we come to know any truth.

When I present this concept to my students, I use the example of an onion. I tell them to think of the truths of the faith present in the center of the onion. It becomes the task of each generation to peel away a layer at a time, thereby receiving deeper insights to those truths. Or think of any basic truth of life and how we come to understand it more fully. No one today would espouse the validity of slavery or seriously consider rescinding the voting rights of women in the United States. Did the owning of another human being or the treating of one half of the human race differently suddenly become wrong? Or was it always wrong? Were they always truths that humanity would finally come to see clearly through a process of growth and development?

So too with God's Revelation. The truths revealed by God are there for humanity to come to know, understand better, and then be articulated for a new generation. Think of the dogma of the Incarnation, the truth of the faith that holds that the Son of God took on the human condition and walked among us at a particular time in history. For the last 2,000 years, humans have been fascinated by the question: Why did God become human? And if you study the history of theology, you will find numerous theological responses to this question as theologians peeled away the layers to get deeper insights into this mystery, and then to find ways to speak about it to a new generation in a way that will have meaning in their lives.

87. What new methodologies have theologians employed since the Second Vatican Council?

After Vatican II, theology took a more practical turn. The new theologians set a new agenda, moving from an old, rather more speculative formula—"faith seeking understanding"—to a more wholistic goal that was already established in the primitive church. They cited the instruction from 1 Peter 3:15–16: "Always be ready to make a defense to anyone who asks for the reasons for the hope that is in you, and make it with modesty and respect." Leaning on this passage, Congar, Chenu, and de Lubac presented their own challenge to theologians who would follow them into the new millennium. They insisted that theologians of every era have always had the same task: to mediate the gospel within the context of their own age. According to theologian Joseph Komonchak, the theologians of the patristic period and the medieval period were successful in mediating the gospel for their time. Unfortunately, generations that came after Aquinas failed to repeat the successes of previous ages.

Joseph Komonchak claims that instead of launching a new, confident evangelizing effort within the new cultural context (like the Renaissance and the Enlightenment), the church created a distinct Catholic subculture and, within that closed world, proceeded to talk only to itself. The leaders of that subculture moved those in priestly training from the universities to seminaries, where they asked questions that had been asked before and answered them with a method and a language familiar only to them. In effect, theology was being done in a vacuum with little or no input from the culture it was intended to serve ("Defending Our Hope: On the Fundamental Tasks of Theology," in *Faithful Witness,* edited by Leo J. O'Donovan and T. Howland Sanks [New York: Crossroad, 1989], pp. 14–26).

Then came Vatican II. The great conciliar theologians, primarily the *periti,* recalled for the Council Fathers the church's two great historic efforts to face the cultural challenges of their day—the patristic and the Thomistic—both of which differed so remarkably from the church's state of siege retreat from the surrounding culture of the last 150 years. They implied that the church could and should attempt to do in the future what it had done so well in the distant past.

The Fathers of Vatican II responded by writing a new charter for the future of theology in the church. Theologians should try to articulate the meaning of the gospel, with language that their contemporaries could understand, to those inside the church as well as to "the others" outside. They were encouraged to develop a theology of reception, meaning that theologians had to relate the meaning of the gospel to demands for meaning and value that were coming out of the surrounding culture.

This did not mean that the gospel would be tailored to fit the expectations and demands of modernity—change for change's sake. The gospel has its own demands; it would meet the questions that inquiring minds brought to it, but it would also transform their horizons, leading them to ask questions they hadn't asked before. To do this, theologians would have to analyze how the modern mind works and then try to show how that modern mind is open to the question of God and the possibility that God might be speaking also to them as they reflect on who they are and why they are here—in other words, to men and women who are caught up in a search for meaning, truth, and goodness.

Post-Vatican II theology would take a leap from the abstract to the concrete, from doing theology deductively to using the inductive approach.

88. What do you mean by the inductive approach to theology?

The task of a theologian is to study the divine-human relationship. Who is God? How does the human come into contact with this God? Before Vatican II, theologians employed a deductive methodology in this endeavor. They would begin a study of the divine partner. This resulted in a list of attributes for God. God is all good, God is all forgiving, and so on. At that time we also read the Bible literally and, unfortunately, we came across a line in scripture that said: "Be perfect as your heavenly Father is perfect." So we assumed that humans must strive to be just like God. But that is impossible. God is God; we are not. This approach certainly contributed to long lines at the confessional every Saturday! Catholics felt a good deal of frustration and guilt—there simply was no way to measure up to the demands of Catholicism at the time. Many even gave up trying. This approach did not take the human condition into consideration as a genuine source in the theological endeavor. But theologians attuned to the working of the Spirit in our lives were preparing a different approach to the "doing" of theology. They came to understand that if the gospel is to take root in the hearts and souls of humans, then they must understand the basic needs and desires of the human person. Theologian Joseph A. Komonchak puts forward two basic questions in this regard: "What must be true about human beings if the gospel of Jesus Christ is addressed to them as a message of salvation? What must be true about them if it is *his* word which they have needed and his cross and resurrection which has redeemed them?" He claims it is not possible to articulate the meaning of the Christian gospel without considering the persons to whom and for the sake of whose salvation it is preached (Joseph A. Komonchak, "Defending Our Hope: On the Fundamental Tasks of Theology," in *Faithful Witness,* edited by Leo J. O'Donovan and T. Howland Sanks [New York: Crossroad, 1989], p. 21). The very opening lines of *Gaudium et Spes,* the Pastoral Constitution on the Church in the Modern World, reflect this inductive approach to theology: "The joys and the hopes, the griefs and the anxieties of the men of this age, especially those who are poor or in any way afflicted, these too are the joys and hopes, the griefs and anxieties of the followers of Christ. Indeed, nothing genuinely human fails to raise an echo in their hearts.... Therefore, the Council focuses its attention on the world of men, the whole human family along with the sum of those realities in the midst of which that family lives." The Council Fathers understand that for the church to be in dialogue with the people of God, it must take seriously the world in which these people live and breathe and have their being. Only then can the message of the gospel have real meaning; only then can this message take root.

89. So what should post-conciliar theologians be doing today?

Given the tension experienced by theologians today, both amongst themselves and in their relationship to the magisterium, this topic still requires serious study, genuine discernment and, I might add, a good deal of patience. In our attempt to understand exactly what theologians are supposed to be doing, Dominican theologian Aidan Nichols provides an excellent starting point (Aidan Nichols, O.P., *The Shape of Catholic Theology* [Collegeville, Minn.: Liturgical Press, 1991], pp. 28, 32). He claims there is a tendency in some circles to dismiss the rational claims of theology. After all, some might say, the finite human is incapable of fully comprehending the mystery who is God. Quite true. But, borrowing an insight from another Dominican, Thomas Aquinas, Nichols says that faith has an inbuilt tendency toward the vision of God and this faith moves toward more clarity, toward intellectual union with its God. The catechism answer comes to mind: "God made me to know him, love him, serve him...." I was created to come to know my God. And so, faith must permit continuous understanding of what it believes. Theology can bring us this growth in understanding. Secondly, there are those who hold that a theologian's task is simply to articulate whatever the voice of church authority determines to be true. Of course, it goes without saying that theologians do have the responsibility of defending and explaining the defined teaching of the church. But they have an even broader responsibility. They must put ever new questions to our shared faith.

Nichols then gives what I consider to be the best definition of theology that I have ever seen. He says it is "the disciplined exploration of Revelation." Each element of this definition is critical. First, the task of theology is disciplined. As a theologian, I am not free to say whatever I want and teach it as true. Rather, I am bound by the formal sources of Revelation: Scripture, and Tradition. They become a kind of yardstick by which I measure the credibility and the veracity of my insights. And yet, the task involves exploration. Theology is not simply the reassertion of something that is already taught or obvious to all believers. It seeks to probe what is already known in the hope of yielding even deeper insights and new applications for Christian living. Finally, theology is interested in coming to know and understand better what God has revealed. It begins by presupposing the truths of Revelation or, as Nichols claims: "Theologians consecrate themselves to the meaning of Revelation." And this consecration to the meaning of Revelation must take seriously new questions, new data, new discoveries of each age. Again, *Gaudium et Spes* supports this point. In Article 62 we read: "Furthermore, while adhering to the methods and requirements proper to theology, theologians are invited to seek continually for more suitable ways of communicating doctrine to the men [and women] of their times. For the deposit of faith or revealed truths are one thing; the manner in which they are formulated without violence to their meaning and significance is another." The last part of this quote comes directly from Pope John XXIII's opening address to the Council on October 11, 1962.

Why have I given such attention to the task of theology? For one thing, there are many in the church who are honestly unaware of this task. The other reason is this: there is a very serious conflict today between theologians and the magisterium, a reality that has caused much suffering in the church, especially since Vatican II.

90. What is the *magisterium?*

This is what we call the teaching office of the church, comprised of the pope and the bishops. The word *magisterium* is taken from a Latin word, *magister,* meaning "teacher." As such, the hierarchy is called to a service in the church. Catholicism holds that the bishops are the successors to the apostles. However, in light of this discussion, it is important to note that there is no indication that

Jesus spelled out in any detail how the local communities were to be structured. In fact, a careful reading of the New Testament indicates that church structure developed only later. Thus, fixed patterns of ministry were not laid out from the very beginning but rather, as the needs in the church arose, new forms were developed to meet these needs. (This practice might be something the contemporary church could take another look at, given the shortage we are currently experiencing in vocations to the priesthood and religious life.) As the early church began to spread, it was challenged by the need to preserve its unity by various heresies emerging at the time. A solution gradually came about: a commissioned authoritative ministry was developed; a list of authoritative apostolic writings was issued; and a common creed was drawn up. By the year 150 or so, the system of a monarchical episcopate (one bishop as the official leader in a local community) was pretty much established. They saw this as a way of guaranteeing the church's tradition. This principle is still in place today. But contemporary Catholicism's understanding of the magisterium owes a great deal to developments that occurred during the Middle Ages, which tended to place more and more power in the bishop of Rome, the pope. It reached a high point at the First Vatican Council (1869–1870) that defined papal primacy and papal infallibility. This primacy given to the papacy at Vatican I placed all church authority basically in the hands of the pope. What this all meant was not very clear at the time. Vatican I had planned a fuller discussion of authority in the church, but was prevented from doing so because of a possibility of a war between France and Germany.

91. Did Vatican II have anything to say about the *magisterium?*

Yes. Chapter III in *Lumen Gentium,* the Dogmatic Constitution on the Church, discusses the hierarchical structure of the church with special reference to the episcopate (the body of bishops). The magisterium has a twofold task: to proclaim the truth and to defend the truth against error. Article 25 states: "They are authentic teachers, that is, teachers endowed with the authority of Christ....By the light of the Holy Spirit, they make that faith clear, bringing forth from the treasury of Revelation new things and old, making faith bear fruit and vigilantly warding off any errors which threaten their flock." And in *Dei Verbum,* the Dogmatic Constitution on Divine Revelation, we read that the bishops have the task of "authoritatively interpreting the Word of God," which theologian Francis Sullivan, S.J., well known for his work on the magisterium, explains as the task of discerning the consistent patterns and general directions that the Scripture gives in matters of Christian faith and practice. However, it is essential that there be a healthy and open dialogue between the official teachers of the church and theologians because, as Father Sullivan maintains, "the work of theologians is no less an ecclesial ministry than that of the bishops. They are both engaged in a ministry to the Word of God." (Included in this task is the guarding, understanding, explaining, teaching, and defending of the faith.) The theologian is to be seen as a mediator between the magisterium and the people of God. Pope Paul VI gave voice to this point in an address to the International Congress on the Theology of Vatican II in 1966. Father Sullivan points to a twofold mediation: from the faith, culture, and questionings of the people to the magisterium; and from the teachings of the magisterium to the people. In that address, Paul VI said: "Without the help of sacred theology the magisterium could no doubt protect and teach the faith: but it could hardly achieve that...profound knowledge which it needs...to perform in a fully satisfactory way" (Francis Sullivan, S.J., *Magesterium: Teaching Authority in the Catholic Church* [New York: Paulist Press, 1983], p. 185). And as noted in *Ad Gentes,* Vatican II's Decree on the Church's Missionary Activity, theologians help the magisterium to know how to preach the gospel more effectively to the people of different cultures.

In recent years, however, this dialogue between theologians and the magisterium has not always been so open and healthy. The cause of the problem, in the eyes of many commentators, has been the exercise of undue control by the bishops. This is unfortunate.

As Father Sullivan points out, if a theologian is to fulfill his or her vocation, freedom is needed to research, to publish, and to teach. *Gaudium et Spes* made this clear as well in Article 62: "Let it be recognized that all the faithful, clerical and lay, possess a lawful freedom of inquiry and of thought, and the freedom to express their minds humbly and courageously about those matters in which they enjoy competence."

92. Overall, what was the Council trying to do and what did it do?

Some hard-line critics of Vatican II said the Council had tried to "Protestantize the church." Liberal commentators laughed over that. There's still no mistaking a Catholic Mass, the whole world over. But the liberal majority at the Council did say that in some ways Vatican II was a long-overdue response to the call for reform launched by Martin Luther in the sixteenth century. Since Rome's corruption had deafened even the pope to that call, Luther seceded from the church and started a movement that rocked the world. History books call it the Reformation, while some Catholic history books called it the Protestant revolt.

But Pope John's favorite word, the Italian *aggiornamento,* (which means "updating"), is, after all, just a more polite word for reform. Insofar as members of the Council majority succeeded in making the church less a church of laws and more a church of love, making it more free, more humble in the face of history, and more at the service of humankind, they probably succeeded in bringing a smile to the face of "St." Luther, looking down from heaven. (John Todd, the late, famous British publisher, who was a good Catholic and a good Lutheran scholar, once tried to promote the cause of Luther's canonization.) Luther would also have applauded the Council's efforts to give the church back to the people.

Before the Council, most Catholics would have defined the church in terms of pope and bishops, priests and nuns. This was the church I grew up in. I can still remember my eighth-grade Sister (no shortage of nuns at that time!) drawing a triangle on the blackboard that described the church. Some of my readers may remember that image. My current students do not. At the top of the triangle was the pope, followed by bishops, priests, sisters, and then, finally, the laity. Truth and authority lay at the top—with the pope. He in turn passed his power down to those below. Those at the bottom of the pyramid had only one imperative—to listen and obediently receive those teachings. (Or, as some have said it, "to pray, pay, and obey.") No one seemed to see the need for dialogue amongst all the members, or consulting the faithful on matters of doctrine (although Cardinal John Henry Newman wrote a famous essay on that subject in 1859).

Some have referred to this pyramid as the CEO model (for Chief Executive Officer). In truth, for some centuries now, popes have tended to function like CEOs (in stark contrast to the New Testament understanding of leadership—that of service). Everyone below the pope receives instructions, doctrine, and direction—as though the popes (and they alone) are in full possession of the truth. Critics of Pope John Paul II's papacy have made such charges. But this modus operandi is not the "creation" of this pope. He inherited it, as it predates him by many years. In 1956, Yves Congar, the French Dominican theologian who was to become one of the leading lights of Vatican II, wrote his mother a note after he and many of his fellow Dominicans in France had been silenced by the Vatican. He was speaking of Pope Pius XII when he wrote:

> The present pope has developed almost to the point of obsession a paternalistic regime: he and he alone should say to the world what it has to think and what it must do. He wishes to reduce theologians to commentating on his statements and not to dare to think something or undertake something beyond mere commentary (Yves Congar, "Silenced for Saying Things Rome Didn't Like to Have Said," in *National Catholic Reporter,* June 2, 2000).

There is no basis for such a model of the church in the New Testament. In fact, when the Fathers of Vatican II looked to the early church for a guide to their reform, they were inspired by Congar himself and his fellow Dominican, M. D. Chenu, who made a case for going back to sacred Scripture and the primitive Christianity of the Fathers of the Church for guidance in the future church.

In fact, this was one of the standing orders for those writing the Council documents: "return to the sources." By this, they meant that over the years the church had taken on any number of accretions, or overlays, like the barnacles on the bottom of a boat, that had little or nothing to do with the gospel. They believed it was time to scrape off the barnacles on the barque of Peter and return to a simpler faith. They could do that, they said, by going back to the New Testament and letting the words of Jesus and the apostles guide us in our journey toward salvation.

Two developments in particular are significant. At the Council, the Fathers chose to "describe" the church in most biblical and theological terms, rather than "define" it in classic legalese. They settled upon three images: the church as "mystery," the church as "sacrament," and "the pilgrim church."

93. What do you mean by the church as "mystery"?

Can we do a little history here? Let's go back to the Reformation, triggered in large part by Martin Luther, a rather learned Augustinian monk with a good theological education. This was a time in history when most priests had little or no theological expertise, simply because the church didn't yet have the seminary system that it would soon put in place to battle the likes of Luther. The average priest was simply no match for Luther. And so, at the Council of Trent (1545–1563), the Roman Church decided it would build seminaries for the training of priests and develop a huge compendium of questions and answers about the faith (called a catechism). That catechism was designed as a kind of defense: if we knew all the answers, then nothing like a Protestant Revolt could happen again.

As a result, however, the church developed a rigid mentality, seeking security in a set of certain propositions that Catholics had to believe or be damned. It was not a mentality that was at all open to dialogue, or to a gentle seeking after the truth by folks who believed in Jesus but might have differing views on how they might follow him. No. The Roman Church became more and more like a bank, with a vault full of unchangeable truths, and a team of officers and guards to watch over it. The church even had a special term for it: "the deposit of faith."

Vatican II would change this by its discussion of the church as "mystery." The Church of Christ is more than a mere human organization. It is not like the Boys' and Girls' Club of America, begun by humans and guided by humans. No, we believe that the church was divinely founded and continues to be guided by the presence of the Holy Spirit. As such, it is more than simply a human reality. It is, in the words of the Fathers, truly a mystery—a combination of the human and the divine. In this sense, then, the use of the word "mystery" is a recognition of this fact. God is present in the church and the infinity of God simply transcends the human's ability to have all the answers. Describing the church as "mystery" leads to a humble approach in our search for the truth and a certain tentativeness in our journey toward the fullness of truth, who is God. This means we can no longer claim to have all the answers. This fact should not worry us. It is simply an acceptance of our humanity, a humanity lovingly fashioned by its God.

94. What do you mean when you say that the Council Fathers described the church as "a sacrament"?

The Council of Trent decreed seven sacraments for the church: baptism, confirmation, eucharist, penance, marriage, holy orders, and the anointing of the sick, and defined sacraments as outward signs intended to give grace, that is, to make God present in our lives. At Vatican II, the Fathers began to think about this and realized that the church helps to do this, too. It helps make God present to the world. And so, one of the major developments to come from the Council was the designation of the church as "the sacrament of salvation." Just as Jesus was the Sacrament of the Father, the church is the sacrament of Christ. It continues the salvific activity begun by the historical Jesus. But we should not forget that this saving activity is not confined to the institutional church, but something that is carried on through time by all Christians, by the people of God. The body of Christ is the body of the church. This was not a latter-day invention: Pope Pius XII wrote an encyclical on it in 1943. It was called *Mystici Corporis,* a title that referred to the mystical body of Christ, that is, the church.

95. How did the other Christian churches react to this notion that the church was a "sacrament"?

Lutherans wondered if the Roman Catholic Church was veering over (again) into triumphalism. To be triumphant is a good thing. It means you won. But triumphalism is not a good thing. Generally, it connotes the behavior of a poor winner, someone who gloats over an achievement. And, in many ways after the Reformation, the Catholic Church was perceived as triumphalistic, viewing itself as the only true church, the only portal to salvation. An examination of pre-Vatican II catechisms clearly demonstrates this where one finds many critical, negative statements about other Christian churches. Naturally, then, the Lutherans and others were concerned when Vatican II started to use the term "sacrament" about itself. They feared it would lead to a divinization of the Roman Church. But a careful reading of the documents and the teachings of those present at the Council should put minds at ease in this regard. The phrase that is used is: "The Church is *like* a sacrament" and functions as such only insofar as the church recognizes her total dependence upon the grace of Christ. As in Article 1 of *Lumen Gentium,* the Dogmatic Constitution on the Church: "By her relationship with Christ, the Church is a kind of sacrament or sign of intimate union with God, and of the unity of all mankind." Again, in Article 9: "God has gathered together as one all those who in faith look upon Jesus as the author of salvation and the source of unity and peace, and has established them as the Church, that for each and all she may be the visible sacrament of this saving unity." The church as sacrament also appears in the Constitution on the Divine Liturgy, *Sacrosanctum Concilium:* "Liturgical services are not private functions, but are celebrations of the Church, which is the 'sacrament of unity'" (Article 26). Seen as coming from Christ, the church is understood as enduring expression of his own graced presence in the world. She is the visible continuation of the invisible Christ.

96. Tell us more about the image of the church as "the pilgrim people of God."

Classic Roman textbook theology before Vatican II presented the Roman Catholic Church as "a perfect society" and claimed all kinds of prerogatives for itself in relation to every other human institution on earth, which contributed to a kind of smugness and arrogance on the part of some members. The Fathers at the Council had another view of the church—as the pilgrim people of God, making their zigzag course through human history, sometimes getting it right, often getting it wrong, but staying the course. This mindset is the opposite of arrogant. It is modest; it is humble; it is self-effacing. And it embraces an old idea—*Ecclesia semper reformanda*—that the church is always in need of reform. This is true because the church on earth is comprised of humans and will therefore always bear the marks of human frailty, weakness, imperfection, and sinfulness. It will also bear marks of great achievement, as its long history of service demonstrates.

But we can never forget the reality of the human condition. When Lord Acton wrote that "power tends to corrupt and absolute power corrupts absolutely," he was writing about a corrupt pope (Roland Hill, *Lord Acton* [New Haven and London: Yale University Press, 2000], p. 300). Other Actons could have written as pointedly about other popes. In attempting to bring the church back to its primitive beginnings, the Fathers of Vatican II were all too aware of past abuses, often done in the name of the church. They wrote in *Gaudium et Spes:*

> Although by the power of the Holy Spirit the Church has remained the faithful spouse of her Lord...still she is very aware that among her members, both clerical and lay, some have been unfaithful to the Spirit of God...it does not escape the Church how great a distance lies between the message she offers and the human failings of those to whom the Gospel is entrusted.(No. 43)

This statement is remarkable. In recent years, Catholics have become aware of the shocking behavior on the part of some clergy. I am referring to cases of child molestation by the clergy. Pre-Vatican II Catholics grew up with the solid image of priests and nuns being perfect, closer to God than anyone else in the church by virtue of their state in life. It was simply taken as a given. But priests and nuns are human beings; and like all humans, they can miss the mark, often widely. But our previous sense of their set-apartness prevented us from realizing this. The leadership in the church before the Council did little to change this perception. It was all too common for a bishop to transfer a priest-pedophile to another parish rather than send him off for treatment, or defrock him. And so, when we first read this admission in *Gaudium et Spes* of past failings on the part of clerics and laity, we were a little stunned. I believe it was a moment of grace for the church. That admission was, no doubt, the foundation for the historic "mea culpas" offered by Pope John Paul II before and during the Jubilee Year celebrations of the year 2000.

I think the pope was only resonating with contemporary disappointment, discouragement, and confusion among Catholics in many parts of the world, particularly among our younger members. This, along with a number of other factors, has contributed to a "credibility crisis" for the institutional church. I hear it frequently from my students. They believe in God but they do not see the institutional church as something they can commit to. I tell them they need to remember that the promise of Christ to be with his church is stronger than any human failing, any human weakness, any human evil. I tell them that we know the official church has at times become a haven for undesirables, but that we will never let the undesirables wear us down. I tell them that we need to believe that the risen Christ will be with us, "even to the end of the world." And that the Holy Spirit "will teach us everything we need to know." And I tell them that the author of those lines is the person who wrote the Fourth Gospel, and that they were written before there was a dividing line between clerics and laity. So the words presumably apply to all the members of the "pilgrim church" who are on their way to the truth. But it took a Vatican II to give the church a solid beginning for a genuine theology of the laity.

97. What is "the theology of the laity"?

Lumen Gentium, the Dogmatic Constitution on the Church, described the laity as all those members in Christ, with the exception of those who are consecrated by religious vows in religious orders and those who have been ordained to the priesthood (No. 31). Prior to the Council, the laity had little, if any, input in church matters. The institutional church was hierarchical and authoritarian. However, given society as a whole before Vatican II, the church's authoritarian status was understandable. The church is a part of society and as such frequently mirrors societal developments. And society at the time was permeated by an authoritarian thinking. Rarely did we question doctors, police officers, teachers, parents, and definitely not priests and nuns! Many a parent heard more than once from their young school age children: "But Sister said…!" The assumption was that if Sister said something, it must be right!

Societally, this all changed in the 1960s, which was a period of great unrest and protest. The Second Vatican Council was just beginning in Rome at the time and was bound to be affected by such an enormous shift in society. There were no laypeople at the Council's first session, and only seven nonclerics at the second session, six of them nuns. At the fourth and final session, there were 52 lay auditors, 29 men and 23 women, including 10 nuns. As auditors, they could listen, but were generally not invited to speak.

But there was another reason why the status of the lay person changed at Vatican II, a profoundly theological reason. As early as 1950, Catholic publications began to speak about a theology of the laity. Theologians like Congar, Schillebeeckx, and Rahner were at the forefront of this movement and they provided a rich framework for the Council Fathers to draw upon. The basic principle underlying their work on the laity was this: the church consists of all baptized members. All have been given the gift of the Holy Spirit. Hence, the laity truly share in the mission and ministry of the church. They are not merely "helpers" of the hierarchy. Rather, through the power and gifts of the Holy Spirit the laity not only have a "direct share" in the work of the church—they *are* the church. The hierarchy is in place not to dominate over the laity, but to serve the entire people of God. The hierarchy is not in place to tell the people of God what they must believe; the hierarchy is in place to witness and proclaim what the people of God *do* believe. Vatican II endorsed this notion, developed more than a hundred years before by Cardinal John Henry Newman in a book-length essay called "On Consulting the Faithful in Matters of Doctrine." His notion is summed up in the Latin term, *sensus fidelium.*

98. What do you mean by *sensus fidelium?*

It is usually translated as "the sense of the faithful." The church must not be understood fundamentally as an institution, where all truth and authority comes from the top down. The theology of the laity holds that the Holy Spirit is active in the whole church. The teaching on "the sense of the faithful" is meant to show that the church's teachings emerge from the faith of all the members. Theologian Miguel Garijo-Guembe has discussed this concept at great length. He points first to the teaching of *Lumen Gentium,* the Dogmatic Constitution on the Church, No. 12, which presents the participation of the entire people of God in the prophetic office of Christ: "The body of the faithful as a whole...cannot err in matters of belief...[for] by this sense of faith, which is aroused and sustained by the Spirit of truth, God's people accepts not the word of men but the very Word of God." Guembe believes this was one of the most important discussions at the Council because it is at the heart of Vatican II's understanding of what it means to be "church." This idea is further supported by history where we can find the Holy Spirit working through charismatic personalities who were not part of the institutional structure [either bishop or pope]. He then raises an important question: "Would it be imaginable that a final decision of the teaching authority would be rejected by the people of God?" He answers with a reference from No. 25 in *Lumen Gentium:* "To the resultant definitions [of the magisterium] the assent of the Church can never be wanting, on account of the activity of that same Holy Spirit." The same Spirit who guides the bishops is present in the members as well (Miguel Garijo-Guembe, *The Communion of the Saints* [Collegeville, Minn.: Liturgical Press, 1994] p. 182).

99. But haven't there been times when the *sensus fidelium* has failed to concur with a teaching of the official church?

First, a little background. This question has to do with a concept called "the doctrine of reception," which has received more attention since Vatican II. Basically, it refers to how well a teaching has been "received" by the whole church. And it is based on the premise that the same Spirit who is present in the official teachers in the church is present in the members as well. If understood correctly, reception of doctrine should demonstrate the interdependence between hierarchical authority and the body of the faithful with regard to church teachings. This mutual reciprocity between those holding office in the church and the community is an essential principle in ecclesiology primarily because of its New Testament roots. The relationship between the founders of the earliest church communities and the members was such that we are told in the Acts of the Apostles that the apostles and the elders made their decision with the entire community (Acts 15:22).

Now, to the question raised above. I believe the honest answer is yes, there have been occasions where the *sensus fidelium* has been unable to support a teaching of the official church. But some clarification is needed here. First, it should be noted that the doctrine of reception does not exclude the possibility that the entire church might need more time (and education) before it can identify with the decisions of the teaching authority and recognize them as useful for its life. Secondly, this discussion refers only to those teachings that have been set forth by the magisterium as non-infallible, or at the level of ordinary magisterium. (Extraordinary magisterial statements deal with teachings directly from Revelation and cannot be rejected.) And, there have been instances in the history of the church where previous decisions made at this level of ordinary magisterium have been revisited and reversed, such as the teaching that only Roman Catholics can be saved. Perhaps the most well-known official teaching that could serve as an example of "non-reception" on the part of many in the church was Pope Paul VI's 1968 encyclical *Humanae Vitae,* which reiterated the church's official ban on artificial contraception.

100. If you could recommend a reading of only one of the sixteen documents of Vatican II, which one would it be?

I am afraid my answer reflects a personal bias. I would recommend *Gaudium et Spes,* the Pastoral Constitution on the Church in the Modern World.

This document did not originate in the preparatory commissions before the Council began. Rather, it emerged directly out of discussion that took place on the floor of the Council. On December 4, 1962, Cardinal Suenens urged the Council Fathers to find a central vision that would articulate how the church understood its relationship to the world. His suggestion was endorsed the next day by Cardinal Montini, who within the year would become Pope Paul VI.

However, much of the impetus of *Gaudium et Spes* can be traced back to John XXIII. In fact this document represents him much more directly than any other Council document. I say this because Suenens' call for a central vision had already been expressed by John XXIII in his opening speech to the Council.

Gaudium et Spes represents what many think is the most profound change from being a church in conflict with the world to being a church seeking to make a contribution to the world. It demonstrated a new consciousness in the church. Theologian Hans Küng has commented that the church at the Council and in this document show the church in a new light. It was a church in the direction of progress and serious renewal, a church no longer fearful of dialogue. And, like John XXIII, *Gaudium et Spes* addressed itself to the whole of humanity with a desire to engage them and the world at large in a genuine dialogue. This dialogue would begin by focusing on the human person. If the church is to make a real contribution to the world, it will have to understand that world.

Now membership in the church came to be seen as integrally linked to a concern for social justice, peacemaking, and the dignity of the human person—all human persons. As Karl Rahner once remarked, at Vatican II the Catholic Church really did become a world church—not because it had missionaries all over the world, but because the church embraced all of humanity and offered to all the universal message of the gospel.

The final draft of *Gaudium et Spes* passed with 1,710 votes in the affirmative; 480 of the Council Fathers voted against it.

NINE

EPILOGUE

101. Can anyone make a case for calling another council—Vatican III, perhaps?

There are two major issues facing the church today. Perhaps they will not be given adequate attention by any other instrumentality in the church short of an ecumenical council. They are: (1) collegiality, and (2) the role of women in the church.

It was hoped that Vatican II would complete the work begun at Vatican I, especially with regard to the relationship between the pope and the bishops. The word that describes their ultimate goal is collegiality, which is a kind of code word for more democracy in the church, or, at least, a greater sharing by the bishops, with the pope, in the governance of the universal church. By its emphasis on the need to work out the implications of collegiality, Vatican II, to a certain degree, corrected Vatican I. However, based on certain developments since Vatican II ended, one has to wonder whether a genuine vision of collegiality has been developed or, more importantly, whether Vatican II's vision has been borne out in the concrete lived experience of the church. Furthermore, few of those who advocate more collegiality in the church have written much about the duty of bishops to be collegial with their own priests and people.

Judging by the theological voices that have been raised regarding this topic, it seems clear that the concept of collegiality must be included as a matter of unfinished business.

So is the question of women in the church. Are women part of the church, or aren't they? A ranking, very crusty theologian in Rome says (privately, because Pope John Paul II considers the issue of women in the church a settled issue): "If they don't want to ordain 'em, then they shouldn't baptize 'em."

The Second Vatican Council opened its first session on October 12, 1962, with a group of over 2,400 cardinals, bishops, abbots, theologians—all men! It would not be until the second session that some women would receive invitations to be auditors for the remaining Council sessions. This was after Cardinal Leo Josef Suenens of Belgium urged his fellow bishops to invite women to attend the Council as auditors, commenting: "Unless I am mistaken, women make up one half of the world's population" (Xavier Rynne, *Letters From Vatican City: Vatican Council II (Second Session)* [New York: Farrar, Straus and Comapny, 1964], p. 117). Looking back with twenty-first-century eyes, it is really hard to conceive how a meeting that would affect the whole church could be held without female representation! But, in fairness, it would be equally hard to conceive of the United States electoral system without the female vote, as was once the case. So women have come a long way in a very short time, more so in the United States than in any other part of the world. Many Catholic women would claim that they have not come far enough. Why is this so? What do women want?

In an attempt to address these questions, the U.S. bishops decided to write a pastoral letter on the situation of women in the church and they invited a number of women to work with them. However, in the spring of 1985, the national board of the Leadership Conference of Women Religious (LCWR) recommended that the bishops defer the writing of this letter for several years and called upon the bishops to reflect and study the issue of the equality and dignity of women. This report also listed some of the problems facing contemporary women. Among these problems were: patriarchy as a worldview that they believed assumes the alienation of women; the exclusion of women in liturgical worship; the claim that, in general, male clergy and hierarchy relate poorly to women; the fact that women are unable to participate fully in ministry and are excluded from governance in the church. This last concern has, unfortunately, been demonstrated in the recent past and serves as a telling example. In June of 2001, Sr. Joan Chittister, a Benedictine Sister/theologian was invited to speak at a conference that was focusing on female ordination.

Prior to the conference, Joan Chittister's Superior received a letter from the Vatican instructing her to forbid Sr. Joan from speaking at the meeting. Failure to comply could have carried the penalties of expulsion from the Order and excommunication. After much prayer and discernment, both the Superior and Sr. Joan decided not to comply with the Vatican's instruction. So far, no penalty has been incurred by either of them. In fact, the Vatican Press Office announced that the Chittister case was closed. For the first time in the history of the church, a group of Sisters challenged the Roman Curia. And the Curia blinked first.

A 1997 report from the World Union of Catholic Women's Organizations stated that many women leave the Catholic church because the church is insensitive to their desire to participate fully in its life and mission. Granted, the key issue in much of the discussion of women in the church does revolve around female ordination. But the problem is really larger than this one issue. It is a problem that will not die a natural death and it, too, is clearly a matter of unfinished business.

I have discussed at length only two items of unfinished business. Of course, there are others: ecumenical dialogue, social justice, tensions between the hierarchy and theologians, an improved system of religious education, to name a few. The Catholic church has entered the twenty-first century. Can it be a church of promise for the new millennium? Can it make the optimism of the gospel relevant again? Can it spark a renewed enthusiasm for the Second Vatican Council, thereby invigorating a new generation? Can it ease the very real tensions that rock the barque of Peter today? One can hope! And I believe that hope will be all the more productive if it is grounded in a wise piece of advice left to us by Blessed John XXIII: "In essential things, unity; in doubtful things, freedom; in all things, charity."

SECOND VATICAN COUNCIL'S 16 DOCUMENTS AND DATES OF PROMULGATION

Sacrosanctum Concilium, Constitution on the Sacred Liturgy, 12/4/1963.

Inter Mirifica, Decree on the Means of Social Communication, 12/4/1963.

Lumen Gentium, Dogmatic Constitution on the Church, 12/4/1963.

Orientalium Ecclesiarum, Decree on the Catholic Churches of the Eastern Rite, 11/21/1964.

Unitatis Redintegratio, Decree on Ecumenism, 11/21/1964.

Christus Dominus, Decree Concerning the Pastoral Office of Bishops in the Church, 10/28/1965.

Perfectae Caritatis, Decree on Renewal of Religious Life, 10/28/1965.

Optatum Totius, Decree on Priestly Training, 10/28/1965.

Gravissimum Educationis, Declaration on Christian Education, 10/28/1965.

Nostra Aetate, Declaration on the Relation of the Church to Non-Christian Religions, 10/28/1965.

Dei Verbum, Dogmatic Constitution on Divine Revelation, 11/18/1965.

Apostolicam Actuositatem, Decree on the Apostolate of the Laity, 11/18/1965.

Dignitatis Humanae, Declaration on Religious Freedom, 12/7/1965.

Ad Gentes, Decree on the Missionary Activity of the Church, 12/7/1965.

Presbyterorum Ordinis, Decree on the Ministry and Life of Priests, 12/7/1965.

Gaudium et Spes, Pastoral Constitution on the Church in the Modern World, 12/7/1965.

GLOSSARY

aggiornamento: The Italian word used by Pope John XXIII to describe what he hoped the Council would achieve. It means a renewal or, more accurately, a "bringing up to date" of the Catholic Church.

collegiality: The term used by Vatican II to describe the common responsibility that the whole episcopal body (the bishops), under the pope, has with regard to the exercise of authority and teaching in the church.

conclave: The word comes from the Italian phrase *con clave,* "with a key." It refers to the assembly of the cardinals and the place where they gather to elect a new pope. It calls for a strict enclosure of the cardinals, allowing for no contact with the outside world during their deliberations.

council: A group of church officials, scholars, hierarchy, and clergy, called together to discuss or study doctrinal or disciplinary matters pertaining to the church.

curia: As used in the church, the term refers to the center of governance and includes all administrative groups and personnel. The Roman Curia is the entire body of official agencies who assist the pope in the government and administration of the church. The Roman Curia was established by Pope Pius X in 1908.

doctrine of reception: This refers to the way a particular teaching of the magisterium is "received" by the faithful. It understands the whole church as the people of God and emphasizes the connection that exists through the activity of the Holy Spirit between the teaching authority in the church and the members. *Lumen Gentium,* the Dogmatic Constitution on the Church, addressed this concept in Article 25, claiming that the consensus of the church can never fail to agree with the definitions (of the magisterium) due to the effectiveness of the same Holy Spirit given to all the members.

Eastern Rite Churches: These are groups of Christian churches in the East that are in communion with the Roman Catholic Church. They are of the Byzantine Rite and include Catholic Armenians, Chaldeans, Catholic Copts, Ethiopians, Maronites, Catholic Syrians, and those of the Malabar Rite. Each is as fully "catholic" as the Western Church. They retain their own liturgies, canon law, and customs but teach the same faith and morals. Vatican II discussed these churches in *Orientalium Ecclesiarum,* the Decree on the Catholic Churches of the Eastern Rite.

ecumenical: Literally universal—coming from the Greek word meaning "worldwide." It is commonly used to identify the general councils of the church, but it also refers to the movement toward reunification of the separated Christian churches.

encyclical: This is a document issued by popes treating matters pertaining to the general spiritual welfare of the church and circulated to Catholics throughout the world.

eschatological: Eschatology is the study of "the last things." It would include the kingdom of God, judgment, heaven, hell, purgatory, the resurrection of the body, and the Second Coming of Christ.

indefectibility: This is a theological principle grounded in the promise of the risen Christ in Matthew 28:16: "...and lo, I am with you always, to the close of the age." Because of this divine promise and, in spite of the sin of the members who make up the church, error will not have the last word.

magisterium: This is the term used for the official teaching body of the church, comprised of the pope and his brother bishops. The church recognizes two levels of magisterial teaching: (1) Extraordinary, dealing with dogmas of the faith. These include the articles of the Creed, the solemn teachings of ecumenical councils, and the *ex cathedra* (infallible) teachings of the church. Dogmas constitute the church's rule of faith. To reject a dogma is to place oneself outside the communion of the church; (2) Ordinary, dealing with the church's doctrines. These are authoritative but noninfallibly-proclaimed teachings of the magisterium. The presumption on the part of the believer in favor of these teachings is grounded in the authority of the church. However, since doctrines are not proclaimed infallibly, it is possible to revisit these teachings over time and rearticulate them in light of new questions and insights, even to reverse them.

Orthodox Churches: After the schism (a break in Christian unity) of 1054, which resulted from differences between the Greek Church and the Roman Church, this term was used to distinguish those Eastern Churches from Rome. Orthodox theology believes in the centrality of church councils in the life of faith. They are willing to regard the pope of Rome as the chief bishop in Christianity, but they view him primarily as the "first among equals" in the episcopal college and do not assign to him a universal supremacy of jurisdiction.

parousia: Coming from the Greek word meaning "arrival," this word is used to denote the Second Coming of Christ at the end of the world. The earliest Christians believed that the parousia was imminent and this belief is a factor that biblical scholars take into account in their interpretation of the biblical texts.

peritus: This comes from the Latin word meaning "expert" and was the term used for those theologian-scholars who assisted the Council Fathers at Vatican II.

pilgrim church: *Lumen Gentium,* the Dogmatic Constitution on the Church, speaks about a church that changes. It introduces the term "pilgrim church," one of the most significant images to emerge from the Council. It implies that, far from being a perfectly complete church, the church after Vatican II recognized itself as journeying "toward" the fullness of truth, who is God.

primacy: Papal primacy means that the pope, by virtue of his office, is the head of the church just as Peter was the head of the apostles. As such, he is to function as the source of unity for all Christians and the protector of the ancient deposit of the faith. Theologically, primacy does not diminish the function of other bishops nor the autonomy of the local church, e.g., diocese.

religious life: From the earliest times in the church, some men and women have responded to the gospel call to be disciples of Christ by living with other Christians in communities gathered together for prayer, ministry, and Christian service. Eventually, many of these communities developed into religious orders who would live the common life and commit themselves to the vows of poverty, chastity, and obedience. This manner of living is referred to as the religious life. Vatican II called these communities to a two-fold renewal: (1) a return to the spirit and charism of the community's founder, e.g., St. Dominic for the Dominicans, St. Ignatius Loyola for the Jesuits; (2) an adjustment of the religious community to the changing conditions of the times.

revelation: God's self-disclosure to humankind through creation, persons, and events. The Catholic Church holds that revelation takes place within the history of God's people reflected in the Old and New Testaments, reaching its fullness in the person of Jesus Christ.

schemata: A Latin word which refers to the documents that were drafted at Vatican II by the Council Fathers.

sensus fidelium: Literally, the "sense of the faithful." The Holy Spirit is active in the whole church. The term indicates that the church's teaching emerges out of the faith of the entire church and is evidence of a mutuality between hierarchical authority and the faithful in the formulation of doctrine.

spirituality: This word is used to describe the different ways in which people experience the transcendent. For Christians, it pertains to the ways we experience life in Christ—the daily unfolding of one's fundamental decision to live the Christian life. The presence of Christ in his church makes possible the general and individual response to God through the gifts of the Holy Spirit.

synod: An official assembly of church leaders to discuss and decide on matters pertaining to doctrine, discipline, or liturgy. Such meetings can occur at the international, national, regional, or diocesan level.

tradition: This is the manner in which Catholics understand and live the teachings of Jesus Christ. Tradition is derived from the creeds of the church, its practice of worship, the writings of theologians, and the teachings of church councils and popes.

SUGGESTIONS FOR FURTHER READING

Document Collections:

Abbott, Walter M., ed. 1966. *The Documents of Vatican II.* New York: America Press.

Flannery, Austin, ed. 1975. *Vatican Council II: The Conciliar and Post-Conciliar Documents.* Northport, N.Y.: Costello Publishing Company.

Accounts and Memoirs:

Brown, Robert McAffee. 1964. *Observer in Rome: A Protestant Report on the Council.* Garden City, N.Y.: Doubleday.

Murphy, Francis. X. 1999. *Vatican Council II.* Maryknoll: Orbis Press.

Stacpoole, Alberic, ed. 1986. *Vatican II by Those Who Were There.* Minneapolis, Minn.: Winston Press.

Studies:

Alberigo, G. and J. Komonchak. 1995, 1997, 2000. *History of Vatican II: Three Volumes.* Maryknoll: Orbis Press.

Doyle, Dennis. 1992. *The Church Emerging from Vatican II.* Mystic, Conn.: Twenty-Third Publications.

Hastings, Adrian, ed. 1991. *Modern Catholicism: Vatican II and After.* New York: Oxford University Press.

McCarthy, Timothy. 1994. *The Catholic Tradition: Before and After Vatican II.* Chicago: Loyola University Press.

Richard, L. et al, eds. 1987. *Vatican II: The Unfinished Agenda—A Look to the Future.* New York/Mahwah, N.J.: Paulist Press.

Schillebeeckx, Edward. 1967. *The Real Achievement of Vatican II.* Trans. H. J. Vaughn. New York: Herder and Herder.

INDEX

Other Books
under the former series title

RESPONSES TO 101 QUESTIONS ON THE BIBLE
by Raymond E. Brown, S.S.

RESPONSES TO 101 QUESTIONS ON THE DEAD SEA SCROLLS
by Joseph A. Fitzmyer, S.J.

RESPONSES TO 101 QUESTIONS ABOUT JESUS
by Michael L. Cook, S.J.

RESPONSES TO 101 QUESTIONS ABOUT FEMINISM
by Denise Lardner Carmody

RESPONSES TO 101 QUESTIONS ON THE PSALMS
AND OTHER WRITINGS
by Roland E. Murphy, O. Carm.

RESPONSES TO 101 QUESTIONS ON THE CHURCH
by Richard P. McBrien

RESPONSES TO 101 QUESTIONS ON THE BIBLICAL TORAH
by Roland E. Murphy, O. Carm.

RESPONSES TO 101 QUESTIONS ON BUSINESS ETHICS
by George Devine

RESPONSES TO 101 QUESTIONS ON DEATH AND
ETERNAL LIFE
by Peter C. Phan

RESPONSES TO 101 QUESTIONS ON ISLAM
by John Renard

RESPONSES TO 101 QUESTIONS ON HINDUISM
by John Renard

RESPONSES TO 101 QUESTIONS ON BUDDHISM
by John Renard

RESPONSES TO 101 QUESTIONS ON THE MASS
by Kevin W. Irwin

RESPONSES TO 101 QUESTIONS ON GOD AND EVOLUTION
by John F. Haught

RESPONSES TO 101 QUESTIONS ON
CATHOLIC SOCIAL TEACHING
by Kenneth R. Himes, O.F.M.

101 QUESTIONS AND ANSWERS ON CONFUCIANISM,
DAOISM, AND SHINTO
by John Renard